לקוטי תורה
וידעת היום

KNOWLEDGE
AND FAITH

לקוטי תורה

וידעת היום

KNOWLEDGE
AND FAITH

a chasidic discourse by
Rabbi Schneur Zalman of Liadi
זצוקללה״ה נבג״מ זי״ע
The Alter Rebbe

•

translated by
Rabbi Eli Kaminetzky

KEHOT PUBLICATION SOCIETY
770 Eastern Parkway / Brooklyn, New York 11213

KNOWLEDGE AND FAITH

CONTENTS

PREFACE

We are pleased to present *Knowledge and Faith*, a Chasidic discourse by Rabbi Schneur Zalman of Liadi, as part of the acclaimed *Chasidic Heritage Series*.

Delivered on *Shabbat Parshat Va'etchanan, Shabbat Nachamu,* 5565 (1805), the discourse discusses the fundamental concept of faith in G-d as compared to the imperative to "know" G-d, and the differences between the two.

The Hebrew text of this discourse was originally published in *Likkutei Torah, Parashat Va'etchanan*.

The discourse was translated and annotated by Rabbi Eli Kaminetzky; editing and additional annotating by Rabbi Avraham D. Vaisfiche.

Thanks are due to *Heichal Menachem*, whose publication of this discourse in the *Chasidut Mevoeret* series aided in its translation and annotation.

Additional thanks are due to Dr. Shmuel Klatzkin, for the Introduction and Summary, to Rabbi Shmuel Simpson for contributing towards the translation of this work, to Rabbis Yosef B. Friedman and Dovid Olidort for their editorial guidance, and to Rabbi Mendel Laine for coordinating the project.

Kehot Publication Society

9 Adar 5773
Brooklyn, New York

RABBI SCHNEUR ZALMAN OF LIADI
זצוקללה"ה נבג"מ זי"ע
5505–5573 (1745–1812)

Facsimile of handwritten manuscript by Rabbi Schneur Zalman

INTRODUCTION
AND SUMMARY

INTRODUCTION AND SUMMARY

FAITH AND KNOWLEDGE: CONFLICT OR ACCORD?

Modern thinkers have employed many words in describing the relationship between faith and knowledge. In the secular culture of the past few hundred years, these two concepts appear to many as irreconcilable opposites. To the rationalist, faith is irrational credulity, something a thinking person replaces with knowledge. To a believer, knowledge is something small and stunted, for the finite human mind is incapable of truly reflecting on the infinite majesty of G-d.

In this discourse, Rabbi Schneur Zalman of Liadi presents the following view. There is no denying that the mind and its elements are gifts from G-d; it is equally true that faith inspires us in a way that mere accumulation of knowledge cannot. Faith's inspiration lifts us beyond the boundaries of our finite existence, yet, that inspiration can depart just as easily as it came. Knowledge, however, becomes a part of us and thus changes us decisively.

In effect, faith and knowledge complement and balance each other.

MOSES' INSTRUCTIONS

This Chasidic discourse is anchored in a Scriptural verse in which Moses tells the Jewish people: *Know therefore today, and take it to your heart that the Lord is G-d in the heaven above and on the earth below, there is no other*[1]. This is not the first verse to speak about knowing G-d. But here knowledge is mentioned in conjunction with a specific time: today. Getting ready to cross over the Jordan River to enter the Land of Israel, Moses tells the people to know something about G-d.

A PRISONER OF INFINITY?

What can we know about G-d? Were He to be locked into infinity, then we would know nothing. Why is this so? Everything about us humans is finite, including our knowledge. If

---

1. Deuteronomy 4:39.

everything about G-d would be infinite, then we would inhabit two worlds which do not touch each other, and not even our knowledge could bridge the gap.

However, the Torah asserts that G-d relates to this world and us who are in it, and that that relationship in no way compromises His transcendence. This world is the handiwork of "The Blessed One who spoke and the world came into being";[2] it is divorced neither from His knowledge nor His being. In fact, His being serves as source of its being, and His knowledge is the source from which our own wisdom flows.

KNOWLEDGE—PARTICIPATION AND CHANGE

So *Know...today*. What we *can* know is G-d as He participates in our days, as He is present within the world that we inhabit and know. G-d is present within the limitations of the world, within time and history, within the place where we are, and within our own human awareness and consciousness. Moses' instructions to the Jewish people are not about things which they have not apprehended or seen. He is speaking when the experience of the Exodus and of the Revelation at Sinai are fresh in the people's memory. He is not referring to philosophical speculation or abstract hypotheses. He is asking the people to reflect on their own experience with G-d, and so, to know what G-d has invested in them and in their mission in the world.

Within the world, one time is not like another; neither is one place nor one person. Each place, time, and person has differences which define them and make them recognizable as just who or what they are. As there is change going from one time, place, or person to another, so, too, the knowledge that pertains to those things will change.

This is true of the knowledge of G-d as well. Certainly, we are not saying that G-d's character changes. But there are some times when we have a vibrant knowledge of G-d and we are very close. At other times, in the world's history or in our own

---

2. Liturgy, Morning Prayer.

personal lives, we are far apart. There was the time of Sinai; not long after, there was the time of the golden calf. There are times when we are filled with the joy of G-d and could not imagine taking a wrong step ever—and there are times when we feel apart and estranged and we walk a troubled path.

If our knowledge of G-d is subject to change in this form, why does Moses bother to ask us to *Know...today*?

THE REALM OF FAITH

There is in fact another mitzvah that addresses a whole different aspect of our own being and our relationship with G-d: the mitzvah of *emunah*—faith. Our relation to those things about G-d which exceed our grasp, His infinity and transcendence is based on faith. We cannot wrap our minds around these intangibles and they do not fit into our experience. In fact, they always exceed our experience. This is the aspect of G-dliness that is called *sovev kol almin*—that which surrounds and encompasses the world and is not contained within it or defined by it.

Since this transcendence is not of our world, it is not subject to change or limitation. It does not come into being when we are in one state of mind and disappear when we are in another. Heaven and earth, dark and light, near and far—all these are indistinguishable with respect to this transcendent aspect. It is even beyond good and evil, as stated in Job (35:6-7), *If you sinned, how did you affect Him?...If you have been righteous, what do you give Him?*

FAITH AS EARTH

The only relation we have with this transcendence is faith. There is no revelation, no experience to grasp. Our intellect cannot help us here. The only faculty we have that has any relation to this transcendence is faith, which is not explicable even to ourselves. It is that mysterious part of ourselves which cannot be reduced to fit into any others. It is not comprehended by the intellect, it is not felt as an emotion. We do not know why we have faith, we have no reason for it.

Yet we stand upon it. And therefore faith is called

"earth"—the most elementary of all things, in that it is inexplicable, but the basis for everything else, all of which is built on its foundation.

NOT OPPOSED TO KNOWLEDGE

We find that faith is not a dead-end, completely opposed to knowledge, but rather the necessary basis for knowledge, for the core of knowledge is something that is not itself known or contained by knowledge. What is the source of the axioms of mathematics? Where does our certainty come from that induction yields reliable fruit? What is the source of our own identity as the one who knows what we know? The answers come only from this extraordinary faculty of faith.

Faith is not in itself an answer, or else it would not be faith. It is as transcendent of the rational mind as the divine reality to which it relates. But faith is not itself confined to one part of our being. It is meant to be filled, even as the divine transcendence in the end is meant to fill.

KNOWLEDGE FILLING THE EARTH

This discourse cites Isaiah's prophecy (11:9) *that the earth will be filled with the knowledge of G-d in this light*: earth—faith—will be filled with knowledge. Just as G-d Himself is not confined to the infinite, so, too, it is with His image in us—He is not to be confined within faith. Just as G-d is a unity of the transcendent and the immanent, both contained and present within the world (*memalei kol almin*) and encompassing and transcending the world (*sovev kol almin*)—so, too, is He present to us both through immanent knowledge and through transcendent faith.

So, our discourse teaches, we apply, using what the prophet describes as G-d's goal, to reveal the nature of our own work in the accomplishment of that goal. There is a knowledge which fills the earth, which is at one with faith. It is this knowledge towards which Moses was directing us—know today within the boundaries of the world, the oneness of G-d.

THE ROLE OF MITZVAH

For that is where Moses continues in his teachings, as the discourse points out. We must *know*, and so G-d revealed Himself to us. But we needed Moses' teachings to comprehend our experience, which had pushed us beyond our limits. So Moses directed us back to something that could be comprehended by us :a mitzvah, something that we can do within the Land, right here in the world: *this is the mitzvah...to do in the Land...flowing with milk and honey. Hear O Israel...G-d is one.*

The first thing that this sequence of verses draws our attention to is the mitzvah—that conjunction of will in which we participate with G-d. Performance of a mitzvah is a tangible expression of the unity of the divine and the human, the dynamic expression of our being created in the divine image. Our participation in this connection gives us a taste of milk and honey, which symbolize a delight in G-d, a taste of bliss. This delight strengthens our connection with the transcendent—it nourishes our faith. In the delight of the mitzvah, we come to understand that our faith is not locked within some realm that is alien to the rest of our life, but that we can live a coherent life in this world centered on G-d.

FROM DELIGHT TO AFFIRMATION: A PALPABLE FAITH

And as the verses roll forward, we are led to the affirmation of the Oneness of G-d—*Shema Yisrael.* In the context of what we have learned, the *Shema* is an affirmation of the oneness of our ineffable faith, what it relates to with our mind and heart, and what they in turn relate to: The Lord, *sovev kol almin*, who is our G-d, in whom we believe by "pure faith," should become one throughout the seven heavens and earth, and so familiar and palpable...to the extent that we can achieve an absolute, selfless devotion and true unity with G-d.

This palpability of G-d's purpose within our life does not just make the transcendent open to our mind and heart. The consequence of having the whole of our being participate in faith is that the latent seeds of love for G-d are nourished. Our faith is expressed with the fire of the heart as well.

END-GAME

Yet still, the discourse cautions, the awakening of an individual to a powerfully nourished faith does not mean the final aim has been reached. How is an individual's strong faith connected to that universal knowledge of G-d which, to Isaiah, is the ultimate goal?

Knowledge, as mentioned before, relates to change. We know things of this world are constantly changing. Our own knowledge of G-d is thus capable of change, and therefore is in need of direction. True, we have known G-d in the past, yet we have strayed, because the knowledge, as a part of the world, reflects our own change.

A strengthened, palpable faith offers unchanging direction that will continually characterize our knowledge, by turning to this faith itself and reflecting its nature, rooted in the ever-present 'I' of G-d, His self, beyond any manifestation.

'I' TO 'I'

The focus on the 'I' of G-d reflects immediately on the 'I' of ourselves. We are moved by our palpable faith to alter our own identity to conform to our source. Here we use *avodah*—working on ourselves, as we actively choose to mold ourselves, through sublimation (*itkafiya*) and transformation (*ithapcha*) of our character, to better reflect who we really are—that divine image.

By building our character on the divine foundation of G-d's 'I,' we attain a constancy, a truly integrated self. In the middle of this world's whirl of time and change, we exhibit through it all an unchanging fidelity backed with a knowledge firmly rooted in the eternal. We uproot all evil in ourselves, with even transgressions becoming merits, so that the Divine Presence will be at home within ourselves and the world entire, the earth upon which faith has made its home.

NOTE ON THE HEBREW TEXT: In vowelizing the Hebrew words in this edition we have followed the grammatical rules of the Holy Tongue, which occasionally differ from the traditional or colloquial pronunciation.

TRANSLATION
AND
COMMENTARY

1.

KNOW THEREFORE TODAY, AND TAKE IT TO YOUR HEART [THAT THE LORD IS G-D IN THE HEAVEN ABOVE AND ON THE EARTH BELOW, THERE IS NO OTHER].[1]

This commandment requires clarification, for is it not already stated, *You have been shown [in order for you] to know [that the Lord is G-d; there is none else aside from Him]*?[2] Why then is it necessary to further command *Know therefore today…*?

Additionally, why does it emphasize *today*?

Now, [this commandment] follows the Giving of the Torah, when the nation [of Israel] encountered G-d *face to face*,[3] and personally heard the Ten Commandments.

"*If we continue to hear [the Lord our G-d's voice we shall perish].*" So they pleaded, "*You* [Moses] *go close and hear [everything G-d will tell you, and speak to us and we will obey].*" G-d agreed to their proposal and said: "*Everything that they said to you is good…Go tell them…*"[4]

[So Moses began dictating G-d's message.] *This is the commandment…to do in the land…a land flowing with milk and honey*; following this it is written *Hear, O Israel, the Lord is our G-d, the Lord is one. You shall love…,*[5] the first commandment which they were given directly by Moses, following the Ten Commandments.

Again, we need clarification: Why does Moses begin by saying *This is the commandment…to do **in the land***, when the commandments listed here are obligations for the individual to fulfill regardless, whether in the land of Israel or not?[6]

KNOWLEDGE AND FAITH

An understanding of all the above requires a clarification of the following concept:

---

1. Deuteronomy 4:39.

2. Ibid., 4:35. When G-d gave the Torah, He opened the heavens and split the lower realms, revealing to the people that He alone is the true existence (*Rashi*).

3. Deuteronomy 5:4.

וְיָדַעְתָּ הַיּוֹם וַהֲשֵׁבֹתָ אֶל לְבָבֶךָ וְגוֹ'.

הִנֵּה יֵשׁ לְהָבִין, הֲלֹא כְּבָר נֶאֱמַר, אַתָּה הָרְאֵתָ לָדַעַת
וְגוֹ'. וּמַהוּ עוֹד וְיָדַעְתָּ?

גַּם מַהוּ הַיּוֹם?

אַךְ הִנֵּה, אַחַר מַתַּן תּוֹרָה שֶׁרָאוּ פָּנִים אֶל פָּנִים וְשָׁמְעוּ
בְּעַצְמָם עֲשֶׂרֶת הַדִּבְּרוֹת,

אָמְרוּ, אִם יוֹסְפִים אֲנַחְנוּ לִשְׁמוֹעַ וְגוֹ' קְרַב אַתָּה
וּשְׁמָע וְגוֹ'. וְהַקָּדוֹשׁ בָּרוּךְ הוּא הִסְכִּים עַל יָדָם וְאָמַר,
הֵיטִיבוּ כָּל אֲשֶׁר דִּבֵּרוּ וְגוֹ' לֵךְ אֱמוֹר לָהֶם וְגוֹ'.

וּכְתִיב, וְזֹאת הַמִּצְוָה וְגוֹ' לַעֲשׂוֹת בָּאָרֶץ וְגוֹ' עַד אֶרֶץ
זָבַת חָלָב וּדְבָשׁ. וּכְתִיב בַּתְרֵיהּ, שְׁמַע יִשְׂרָאֵל הוי' אֱלֹקֵינוּ
הוי' אֶחָד וְאָהַבְתָּ וְגוֹ', שֶׁהִיא הַמִּצְוָה הָרִאשׁוֹנָה שֶׁנִּצְטַוּוּ
אַחַר עֲשֶׂרֶת הַדִּבְּרוֹת מִפִּי מֹשֶׁה.

וְצָרִיךְ לְהָבִין, לָמָּה הִקְדִּים לוֹמַר וְזֹאת הַמִּצְוָה וְגוֹ'
לַעֲשׂוֹת בָּאָרֶץ וְגוֹ', דְּהָא פָּרָשָׁה שְׁמַע חוֹבַת הַגּוּף הִיא
וְנוֹהֶגֶת בֵּין בָּאָרֶץ כוּ'.

וּלְהָבִין כָּל זֶה צָרִיךְ לְהַקְדִּים בֵּאוּר:

4. Ibid., 5:22-27.

5. Ibid., 6:1-5.

6. See *Kiddushin* 37a.

The discourse thus poses three questions.

1. If the people were already shown (and commanded to know) at Sinai that G-d is the L-rd, why is an additional verse and commandment necessary?

2. Why is this commandment limited to "*today*"?

3. If the commandments listed here are universal, why does the verse preface, *This is the commandment to do in the land*? The first and second questions will be answered in ch. 6; the third in ch. 4.

Knowing G-d and having faith in G-d are two separate commandments. It is written, **Know** the G-d of your father (Chronicles 1 28:9) (The term "know" refers to actual knowledge and understanding. *Shaloh, Perek Asarah Maamarot*, Discourse One, explains in similar vein.[7]). It is also written, and they **believed** in G-d.[8] (See *Midrash Rabbah, Beshalach* 23[:5][9] on the verse *Look from the peak of Amana*,[10] and in *Shir Hashirim Rabbah* on the verse, *Come with me from Lebanon*.[11])

MISTAKEN BELIEF

To explain: The common usage of the term "faith," referring to the belief that G-d sustains all life and created the universe from nothing, is mistaken. For this belief, it is not necessary to have "faith," as it is apparent and obvious. Although one cannot see this physically, it is as real as sight.

This is why the verse states, *From my flesh I* **envision** *G-dliness,*[12] as this "vision" is caused by [meditating on] one's flesh: By observing that the body is alive and vibrant, one becomes aware of the soul within him, which is the life force of the body, without which the body cannot remain alive and sustained.[13]

Likewise, one can envision G-dliness through the realization that the universe is comparable to a big body with defined boundries—"From the earth to the [first of the seven

---

7. "The verse *Know the G-d of your fathers* implies that, in addition to the faith instilled within us by our fathers who have passed it down from generation to generation, we must also 'know' G-d using our own intellect."

8. Exodus 14:31.

9. "Rabbi Nechemya said: It was only because of their faith that the Jewish people merited to sing the song at the splitting of the sea.

10. Song of Songs 4:8. The Hebrew word *Amana* is etymologically related

to *emunah*—belief or faith, expressing the following meaning of the verse: *Look at the faith [possessed by the Jewish people] from the very beginning*—i.e., Abraham. It was this faith that caused them to sing at the sea (*Matnot Kehunah; Pirush Maharzav* on the Midrash in the following note).

11. *Shir Hashirim Rabbah* 4:8:2: "In what merit [will the Jewish people be redeemed from exile]? In the merit of their singing at the sea. R. Nachman said: In the merit of Abraham's faith, as the verse states, *and he believed in*

עִנְיַן דַּעַת וְעִנְיַן אֱמוּנָה, שֶׁהֵם שְׁתֵּי מִצְווֹת, כִּי הִנֵּה כְּתִיב דַּע אֶת אֱלֹהֵי אָבִיךָ וְגוֹ' (בְּדִבְרֵי הַיָּמִים א' כ"ח ט'), (דִּרְצוֹנוֹ לוֹמַר בְּחִינַת דַּעַת וְהַשָּׁנָה מַמָּשׁ, וְעַל דֶּרֶךְ זֶה פֵּרַשׁ בְּשַׁלַּ"ה בְּפֶרֶק בַּעֲשָׂרָה מַאֲמָרוֹת מַאֲמָר א'). וּכְתִיב וַיַּאֲמִינוּ בַּהוי' (וְעַיֵּן בְּרֵבוֹת בְּשַׁלַּח פָּרָשָׁה כ"ג, עַל פָּסוּק תָּשׁוּרִי מֵרֹאשׁ אֲמָנָה. וּבְשִׁיר הַשִּׁירִים רַבָּה בְּפָסוּק אִתִּי מִלְּבָנוֹן).

וְהָעִנְיָן, כִּי בֶּאֱמֶת זֶה שֶׁהָעוֹלָם קוֹרִין בְּשֵׁם אֱמוּנָה, לְהַאֲמִין מַה שֶׁהַקָּדוֹשׁ בָּרוּךְ הוּא מְחַיֶּה אֶת כֻּלָּם, וְהוּא בָּרָא אֶת כָּל הָעוֹלָמוֹת מֵאַיִן לְיֵשׁ, טוֹעִים הֵם, שֶׁאֵין צָרִיךְ לָזֶה אֱמוּנָה, שֶׁהֲרֵי זֶה נִרְגָּשׁ בִּבְחִינַת רְאִיָה, הֲגַם שֶׁאֵינוֹ רוֹאֶה בְּעֵינֵי בָשָׂר, הֲרֵי זֶה כְּאִלּוּ רוֹאֶה.

וְעַל זֶה נֶאֱמַר וּמִבְּשָׂרִי אֶחֱזֶה אֱלוֹהַ, אֶחֱזֶה דַּיְקָא. וְהַיְינוּ מִבְּשָׂרִי, שֶׁכְּמוֹ בִּבְשָׂרִי, בִּשְׁבִיל שֶׁרוֹאֶה חַיּוּת הַגּוּף וְקִיּוּמוֹ, יוֹדֵעַ וּמַרְגִּישׁ כִּי נַפְשׁוֹ הִיא בּוֹ, שֶׁהִיא הִיא הַמְחַיָּה אֶת הַגּוּף, וּבִלְעָדָהּ אֵין חַיּוּת וְקִיּוּם לַגּוּף.

כָּךְ אֶחֱזֶה אֱלוֹהַ, מֵאַחַר שֶׁרוֹאִין אֶת הָעוֹלָמוֹת שֶׁהֵם כְּמוֹ גּוּף גָּדוֹל, מֵהָאָרֶץ לָרָקִיעַ מַהֲלַךְ ת"ק שָׁנָה כו'. וְכֵן

G-d. R. Chelbo said in the name of R. Yochanan: It is written, *And the Jewish people saw the great hand of G-d, and they believed in G-d and Moses His servant.* Can it be in the merit of this faith that the Jewish people are redeemed? After all, G-d was leading them by the hand through the sea, so how could they not believe? Is there a man who sees such miracles and does not believe?! Rather in the merit of their earlier faith, while still in Egypt, before they witnessed any miracles, as the verse states, *and the nation believed."*

Thus the discourse has presented two verses, with proof-texts to demonstrate that knowledge and faith are two separate ideas.

12. Job 19:26.

13. By reflecting on the fact that, when the soul departs from the body, the body is left lifeless, one gains a strong conviction that there is a soul which keeps the body alive, although it cannot be seen (*Derech Mitzvotecha* 45a).

heavens] is a five hundred-year journey,"[14] and so on; even spiritual beings such as angels, souls, and so forth are like bodies relative to the energy infused in them from the *Ein Sof*,[15] blessed be He, which creates, sustains and enlivens them.[16]

Thus it is written, *lift your eyes upward and see who created these*[17]: This conviction is as real as "sight," and hence the term "*I envision.*"[18]

DAAT VS. EMUNAH

Therefore, the correct Hebrew term for this concept is not *emunah* [faith], rather *daat* [knowledge], because *daat* is an expression of recognition and intuition.[19]

Additionally, *daat* also indicates an in-depth, unfaltering concentration; bearing a concept in mind diligently, ensuring it will not be forgotten from the heart.[20] Fleeting thoughts, however, cannot accomplish any [change of heart], for "fleeting thought is not like speech."[21]

---

14. *Chagigah* 13a. Nebuchadnezzar said (Isaiah 14:14): *I shall ascend beyond the heights of the clouds; I will be compared to the Most High.* He wished to reach the highest level, the throne of G-d Himself, and be a god. A voice from heaven responded to his arrogant ambition, chastising him by pointing out the vastness of creation and the insignificance of mortal man. (*Be'er Hagolah, Be'er 6* understands the Talmud to be referring to the *spiritual* "distance" between one dimension and the next.)

Yet, although the worlds are vast, as "creations" they are nonetheless defined and limited ("a five hundred-year journey..."). Thus the necessity rises for a *tzimtzum* and a limiting of the *Or Ein Sof.* (See also *Moreh Nevuchim* 1:72.)

15. EIN SOF, in the Hebrew. The Kabbalists use the term *Ein Sof* (lit., "infinite," "endless") to refer to the absolute Infinite force of G-d, totally beyond description, knowledge, and comprehension, beyond any boundaries—the Essence of G-d Himself. (G-d's infinite expression and revelation—the *Infinite light*—is termed, in Hebrew, *Or Ein Sof.*

For as to why the mystics chose to refer to the effusion of Divinity as "light," see *Mystical Concepts in Chassidism,* chapter 1 (*Anthropomorphism and Metaphors*), section 3.)

16. Though an angel is a spiritual being, there still are specific criteria defining the angel's level, mission, and abilities, in its service of G-d. Therefore, they too have a spiritual "body" and a limit to their being. In

אֲפִילוּ דְּבָרִים רוּחָנִים כְּמוֹ מַלְאָכִים וּנְשָׁמוֹת כו', הֵן כְּגוּף
לְגַבֵּי הַחַיּוּת שֶׁבְּתוֹכָם מֵאֵין סוֹף בָּרוּךְ הוּא, הַמְהַוֶּה
וְהַמְחַיֶּה אוֹתָם וּמְקַיְּמָם.

כְּמוֹ שֶׁכָּתוּב, שְׂאוּ מָרוֹם עֵינֵיכֶם וּרְאוּ מִי בָרָא אֵלֶּה,
וִידִיעָה זוֹ מֻרְגֶּשֶׁת כְּאִלּוּ רוֹאֶה כו'. וְזֶהוּ לְשׁוֹן אֶחֱזֶה.

וְלָכֵן אֵין זֶה נִקְרָא בְּשֵׁם אֱמוּנָה בִּלְשׁוֹן הַקֹּדֶשׁ, אֶלָּא
בְּשֵׁם דַּעַת, כִּי דַעַת הוּא לְשׁוֹן הַכָּרָה וְהַרְגָּשָׁה.

וְגַם דַּעַת הוּא הַעֲמָקַת הַלֵּב, שֶׁלֹּא יַסִּיחַ דַּעְתּוֹ מִזֶּה,
וְיִהְיֶה לוֹ לְזִכָּרוֹן לְפָנָיו תָּמִיד, שֶׁלֹּא יִשְׁכַּח וְיָסוּר מִלִּבּוֹ.
מַה שֶּׁאֵין כֵּן הִרְהוּר בְּעָלְמָא לָא עָבִיד מִידֵי, דְּהִרְהוּר לַאו
כְּדִבּוּר דָּמֵי.

---

addition, they are dependent on the infinite G-dly energy that fills them.

17. Isaiah 40:26.

18. In the verse cited above from Job. Consequently, seeing the universe in constant motion also brings us to realize G-d's constant involvement, just as the soul's existence is realized through studying the body.

19. Meditating on the above is a form of fulfilling the commandment to **know the G-d of your father**, as "The knowledge of this is a positive commandment" (*Rambam, Hilchot Yesodei HaTorah* 1:6). "Faith," however, is unnecessary here, for the conviction of G-d's existence is entirely logical.
The discourse continues by de-

fining the term "faith," and describing the circumstances where faith is necessary.

20. One does not need faith to reach a conclusion about G-d's existence and involvement in the world. Nevertheless, one must make the effort to constantly keep this concept in mind in order to ensure that it affects the heart, ultimately making a change in one's behavior. This is indicated by the word *daat*.

21. *Berachot* 20b. Fleeting thought lacks any depth or analysis and therefore has no effect on the person. Speech, however, stirs one's emotions, causing an effect similar to the intuition of *daat*. (See *Or Hatorah, Shir Hashirim*, p. 435.)

2.

BEYOND CREATION

Yet, this form of knowledge and acquaintance can only function at the level of *memalei kol almin.*[22] (This is why the level of
memalei kol almin is called "Revealed World"—as explained in the
discourse beginning *Venikdashti.*[23])

On the level of *sovev kol almin,*[24] however, it is written, *I
am G-d, I have not changed.*[25] (See *Zohar* II, end of *Parshat Terumah,* 176a; III:137b.) And "You are [the same] before the
world was created...."[26]

G-d[27] entirely transcends the realm of the created world,
and it is only G-d's attribute of *malchut*[28] which maintains all

---

22. MEMALEI KOL ALMIN—SOVEV KOL
ALMIN. *Memalei kol almin* is the Divine energy invested within creation.
It permeates all of creation, inter-
acting and responding to the subject
it gives life to. For example, the soul
is clothed within the body in a way
that changes the body fundamentally.
It is the soul which causes the person
to be alive rather than not. See *Sefer
Hamaamarim 5703,* p. 31; *Shaar
Hayichud v'haEmunah,* ch. 6. (See below, fn. 24, for *sovev kol almin.*)

23. *Likkutei Torah, Emor* 31b-c. The
reason being, for it is something that
is *apparent,* as explained above in the
main text regarding the soul and the
body.

24. *Sovev kol almin,* unlike *memalei,*
is the Divine energy that transcends
creation. *Sovev* acts in a remote, in-
direct manner. An analogy: Sunlight
shines into a room and illuminates it
but without any relationship to the
room and its composition. The light
in the room is merely a reflection
from its source in the sun and does

not connect with that which it illuminates. Similarly, the energy of *sovev* is infinite and cannot be confined
within the limits of creation. It therefore "envelops" the worlds in an encompassing and transcending form.
This more subtle light is present, but
remains remote from the object it illuminates. (See *Tanya,* ch. 48; *Sefer
Hamaamarim 5703,* ibid.)

25. Malachi 3:6.

26. "...And You are the same since
the world has been created" (Liturgy,
Morning Prayer).

27. To explain: From the G-dly perspective, the level of *memalei* is G-d as
He interacts with the creation. The
level of *sovev,* however, is G-d as He is
to Himself. Take, for example, a very
wise man who although usually
spends his time involved in deep in-
tellectual thoughts, talks to a very simple person. His interaction with the
simple person is on that person's level,
but the wise man himself is far removed from the simpleton's world.

ב.

אַךְ הִנֵּה דַּעַת וְהַרְגָּשָׁה זוֹ הִיא בִּבְחִינַת מְמַלֵּא כָּל עָלְמִין (וְלָכֵן נִקְרֵאת בְּחִינַת מְמַלֵּא כָּל עָלְמִין בְּשֵׁם עָלְמָא דְאִתְגַּלְיָא כְּמוֹ שֶׁכָּתוּב בְּדְרוּשׁ הַמַּתְחִיל וְנִקְדַּשְׁתִּי בְּתוֹךְ בְּנֵי יִשְׂרָאֵל),

אֲבָל בִּבְחִינַת סוֹבֵב כָּל עָלְמִין כְּתִיב אֲנִי הוי' לֹא שָׁנִיתִי (וְעַיֵּן זֹהַר חֵלֶק ב' סוֹף פָּרָשַׁת תְּרוּמָה קע"ו א', חֵלֶק ג' קל"ז ב') וְאַתָּה הוּא קֹדֶם שֶׁנִּבְרָא הָעוֹלָם כו',

שֶׁאֵינוֹ בְּגֶדֶר עָלְמִין כְּלָל, רַק בְּחִינַת מַלְכוּתְךָ לְבַדָּה

Only because he chose to interact with the simpleton, did the wise man lower himself down to his level. Had he not chosen to do so, the simpleton would not have known of his existence. Furthermore, even while the wise man does interact with the simpleton, he essentially remains aloof and unaffected by him. So, too, to an infinitely greater extent, as far as G-d *Himself* is concerned (i.e., the level of *sovev*), creation causes no change in Him at all. Only because G-d chose to interact with and sustain creation (the level of *memalei*), does the world exist. At the same time, however, G-d *Himself* remains detached and unchanged by the events of the world, even while relating to the world on a certain level, i.e., *memalei*. See *Shaar Hayichud v'haEmunah*, ch. 9; *Iggeret Hakodesh* 5.

28. MALCHUT. The last of the ten G-dly attributes, or *sefirot*, serving as a bridge between G-dliness and the creation. It condenses the divine energy it receives from the earlier nine *sefirot* so that this energy can be properly transmitted down to the beings of creation, tailored to them individually. *Malchut* is the attribute which brings into existence and sustains the world as it is now, as a seemingly independent and separate entity. In a sense, *malchut* is considered to be the "source of life" for all creatures. The earlier *sefirot*, however, remain aloof and detached from creation. They are not a "source of life" or creation in a direct way, due to their lofty state. It is specifically through *malchut* that the creation is brought into being.

Now, since *malchut* is the source of all the created beings—in their seemingly separate and independent state—it therefore is called *malchut*, lit., sovereignty or kingship. For a king receives his title only when he rules over a nation, and is not considered a king over his children, who are merely an extension of himself. Likewise, the earlier *sefirot* are attributes of G-d which are "too close" to Him, and thus not involved with creation. *Malchut*, however, relates to creation in its independent state, and is therefore called "sovereignty." See *Shaar Hayichud v'haEmunah*, ch. 7.

worlds.[29] That is, only a ray and gleam of *malchut* is involved with creation, as it says: *Blessed be the name of the glory of His kingdom for ever and ever*[30]—only the *name* and the *glory* of His kingdom, but not [even] the attribute of *malchut* itself.[31]

Regarding this, our Sages said: "Until the world was created, it was Him and His name alone."[32] Even G-d's name, referring to *malchut*,[33] "alone" and detached from creation, as it says, *for His name is sublimely transcendent, it is unto Himself; [(only) its radiance is upon the earth]*;[34] only a *radiance* and a gleam of *His name* is *upon the earth*.[35] (Regarding this, see the discourses *Lachen Emor LiBnei Yisrael*,[36] *Kechu Me'itchem Terumah*,[37] *Yaviu Levush Malchut*,[38] *U'Vevoah Lifnei Hamelech*,[39] *Shir HaShirim*,[40] and *Kol Dodi*.[41])

---

29. See Psalms 145:13. Aside from the physical world, there are other spiritual worlds, which are considered part of the creation, in the sense that they are independent entities, not merely an extension of G-d Himself. These worlds are generally divided into three, *Beriah*, *Yetzirah*, and *Asiyah*. There is another world above these three, called *Atzilut*, but it is in a state of complete unity with G-d, and is not considered part of the creation. It is the world of the ten *sefirot*. G-d's attribute of *malchut* is the final level in the world of *Atzilut*.

30. See *Pesachim* 56a.

The Hebrew word for "bless" is *baruch*, which can also mean to "elicit." (See this usage in the Mishnah (*Kilayim* 7:1): "One who draws down the branch." See also *True Existence* (Kehot, 2006), fn. 108.) So the verse, *Blessed be the name...*, can be read as follows: "The name of the glory of His kingdom is elicited." I.e., the energy which is elicited below to sustain creation derives solely from the "name" and "glory" of His "king-

dom." The attribute of His "kingdom" itself, however, remains removed from creation. (See *Torah Or, Bereishit* 1d; *Likkutei Torah, Naso* 20d.)

31. See *Creation and Redemption* (Kehot, 2007), pp. 80-86, and footnotes there. "Name" and "glory" are not part of the person's essential character. "Name" is a means for others to refer to him, while "glory" is a result of the impression he makes on others. Similarly regarding *malchut* itself: The essence of *malchut* is "alone" and detached from creation, while the ray of *malchut*—i.e., its name and glory—gives life to creation.

32. *Pirkei d'Rabbi Eliezer*, ch. 3.

33. The fact that until the world was created there existed G-d and His name alone further indicates that the essence of *malchut* itself is too sublime to be involved with creation and only a ray of it animates creation.

34. Psalms 148:13.

הִיא מַלְכוּת כָּל הָעוֹלָמִים, דְּהַיְינוּ בְּחִינַת זִיו וְהֶאָרָה מִמִּדַּת
מַלְכוּתוֹ יִתְבָּרֵךְ, כְּמַאֲמָר בָּרוּךְ שֵׁם כְּבוֹד מַלְכוּתוֹ
לְעוֹלָם וָעֶד, שֵׁם כְּבוֹד מַלְכוּתוֹ וְלֹא מַלְכוּתוֹ עַצְמָהּ.

וְעַל זֶה אָמְרוּ רַזַ"ל [רַבּוֹתֵינוּ זִכְרוֹנָם לִבְרָכָה], עַד
שֶׁלֹּא נִבְרָא הָעוֹלָם הָיָה הוּא וּשְׁמוֹ בִּלְבָד, שֶׁגַּם שְׁמוֹ
הִיא מִדַּת מַלְכוּתוֹ הִיא בִּבְחִינַת לְבַדּוֹ, וּכְמוֹ שֶׁכָּתוּב כִּי
נִשְׂגָּב שְׁמוֹ לְבַדּוֹ, רַק הוֹדוֹ וְזִיווֹ שֶׁל שְׁמוֹ עַל אֶרֶץ כוּ'
(וְעַיֵּן מִזֶּה בְּדֵרוּשׁ הַמַּתְחִיל לָכֵן אֱמוֹר לִבְנֵי יִשְׂרָאֵל, וּבְדֵרוּשׁ
הַמַּתְחִיל קְחוּ מֵאִתְּכֶם תְּרוּמָה, וּבְדֵרוּשׁ הַמַּתְחִיל יָבִיאוּ לְבוּשׁ
מַלְכוּת, וּבְדֵרוּשׁ הַמַּתְחִיל וּבְבֹאָהּ לִפְנֵי הַמֶּלֶךְ, וּבְדֵרוּשׁ הַמַּתְחִיל שִׁיר
הַשִּׁירִים, וּבְדֵרוּשׁ הַמַּתְחִיל קוֹל דּוֹדִי),

---

35. *Likkutei Torah, Shir Hashirim* 38c.

36. *Torah Or, Va'era* 57b: It is written: *For His name is sublimely transcendent, it is unto Himself; (only) its radiance is upon the earth.* "His name" refers to *malchut*—(as it says in the hymn *Adon Olam*) "His name was called king." ...This is the level of *Shechinah*, which descends to the lower worlds, as it is written (Exodus 25:8), *And I will rest within them.* At the same time, the essence of His name still remains transcendent and removed, and there exists an absolute divide between His name and the worlds. It is only a ray of His name that shines upon the worlds.

37. Ibid., *Vayakhel* 88d: There are two levels in the spiritual evolution of the divine light: *memalei kol almin* and *sovev kol almin*. The former is analogous to the soul which gives life to the body; to each specific limb.... Similarly, *memalei kol almin* is the di-vine energy that flows into each specific world in accordance with its needs.... *Sovev kol almin*, on the other hand, is the divine energy that does not actually dwell within the worlds. It is there, but is not invested in them.... A ray of *sovev kol almin* shines forth to produce the level of *memalei kol almin*.

38. Ibid., *Megillat Esther* 90c: G-d's Oneness remains intact just as it was before He created the world. This Oneness is implied by the word *ya-chid*, as opposed to the word *echad*. *Echad* indicates the Oneness found within the seven heavens and four corners of the world, how all of creation is nullified before G-d and is dependent on Him to exist. *Ya-chid*, on the other hand, indicates the true Oneness of G-d, as He ex-isted prior to creation, as He existed as a Singular entity. Even after creation He retains this state of Oneness; it is only from the level of

SOVEV KOL ALMIN

G-d is therefore referred to as One who "encompasses all worlds" [*sovev kol almin*], since all the worlds are insignificant to Him. His divine energy which spreads through the worlds is not analogous to the soul which infuses the body, is sensitive to the body's experiences, and subject to the changes of time, space, temperature, and so on. G-d, though He exists below in the same manner as He exists above, is not beholden to space, heaven forbid. "Below" and "above" are the same to Him.[42]

Now, the meaning of the term *sovev kol almin* is not that G-d is withdrawn from creation; rather, He is found within the worlds as well, although in a transcendent manner.

With this we can explain the phrase, "the Holy, in heaven and on earth."[43] Since He is holy and removed, that is, on the level of *sovev kol almin*, therefore He is on the earth below exactly as He is in the heavens above. (The phrase "the great King,"[44] however, denotes *memalei kol almin*—an expression

---

malchut that the life force is drawn into the world.

39. Ibid., 96a: G-d exists as a Singular entity, far removed from the limitations of the world. And although He is the "life of all worlds," it is only from the level of *malchut*. All the myriad of worlds are derived from a mere ray of His glorious Kingship (*malchut*). But G-d Himself, in all his glory, "cannot be grasped by any mind."

40. *Likkutei Torah, Shir Hashirim* 1c: The source of the world's life force is from His name, i.e., *malchut*. In truth, however, *His name is sublimely transcendent*. Thus, the flowing of divine energy from His name cannot be transmitted in a manner of cause and effect, for then all of creation would

exist in a state of *Ein Sof*. It must go through a process of contraction until its intensity is diminished and it comes forth from *malchut* as a mere "line and thread," along with other forms of contraction and concealment.

41. Ibid., 14c: Our Sages state: "Until the world was created only He and His name existed." The divine energy that gives existence to the world is a mere ray. It is similar to the rays of the sun or a candle which do not affect the light source itself; just as if a curtain blocks the ray the light source is not affected. Similarly, the G-dly force giving life to the world is called "light," since it does not affect G-d and does not cause any change within Him, as the verse states (Malachi 3:6), *I am G-d, I have not changed....*

וְנִקְרָא הוּא יִתְבָּרֵךְ בְּשֵׁם סוֹבֵב כָּל עָלְמִין, שֶׁאֵין
הָעוֹלָמוֹת תּוֹפְסִים מָקוֹם נֶגְדּוֹ, שֶׁחַיּוּתוֹ הַמִּתְפַּשֵּׁט תּוֹךְ
הָעוֹלָמוֹת אֵינוֹ כְּדִמְיוֹן הַנְּשָׁמָה הַמִּתְלַבֶּשֶׁת מַמָּשׁ תּוֹךְ הַגּוּף
וּמִתְפָּעֶלֶת מִמִּקְרֵי הַגּוּף, וּמִמִּקְרֵי הַמָּקוֹם וְהַזְּמַן, קוֹר וְחוֹם
כו', אֲבָל לְפָנָיו יִתְבָּרֵךְ, הֲגַם שֶׁנִּמְצָא לְמַטָּה כְּמוֹ לְמַעְלָה
אֵינוֹ נִתְפָּס בְּגֶדֶר מָקוֹם חַס וְשָׁלוֹם, וּמַעְלָה וּמַטָּה שָׁוִין.

וְאֵין הַפֵּרוּשׁ סוֹבֵב כָּל עָלְמִין שֶׁהוּא מִלְמַעְלָה מִן
הָעוֹלָמוֹת, אֶלָּא הוּא נִמְצָא בְּתוֹךְ הָעוֹלָמוֹת גַּם כֵּן,
וְאַף עַל פִּי כֵן הוּא בִּבְחִינַת סוֹבֵב כָּל עָלְמִין.

וְזֶהוּ וְהַקָּדוֹשׁ בַּשָּׁמַיִם וּבָאָרֶץ, שֶׁלְּפִי שֶׁהוּא קָדוֹשׁ
וּמֻבְדָּל הוּא בְּחִינַת סוֹבֵב כָּל עָלְמִין, לָכֵן הוּא שָׁוֶה
מַמָּשׁ בָּאָרֶץ מִתַּחַת כְּמוֹ בַּשָּׁמַיִם מִמַּעַל (וְהַמֶּלֶךְ הַגָּדוֹל
הַיְנוּ בְּחִינַת מְמַלֵּא כָּל עָלְמִין, הִתְפַּשְּׁטוּת גְּדֻלַּת מַלְכוּתוֹ יִתְבָּרֵךְ,

It is also called "His name." ...Just as a name is not an integral part of a person and is only required for others to call him, similarly the creative force is merely a "name" of G-d and is not essential to His existence at all.... This is the level of *malchut*.... But the essence of G-d is not revealed below (as we say in the Morning Liturgy), "for He alone is exalted and Holy."

42. The term "encompasses all worlds" indicates a level that does not consider a distinction between higher and lower. An analogy: While the people standing on one side of the earth feel that they are on the top, the people on the other side feel that the top is on their side. In truth, however, since the world is spherical, there is neither top nor bottom. Similarly, although a variety of different spiritual levels exist within creation, one more superior than the next, their differences are only significant from the perspective of *memalei kol almin*. From the perspective of *sovev*, however, these divisions are insignificant, for *sovev* encompasses the entire creation from all angles, equally. Hence, the description "surrounds all worlds" indicates that relative to the divine energy of *sovev*, each and every aspect of creation is equally insignificant (*Derech Mitzvotecha* 81a-b).

43. Liturgy, *Yishtabach* prayer.

44. Ibid., immediately prior to the phrase quoted above. The entire sentence reads: "May your name be praised forever, our King, the Almighty G-d, the great and holy King, in heaven and on earth."

of G-d's great kingship, as it is written (Psalms 145:3), *there is no limit to His greatness* and (Daniel 7:10) *A thousand thousands served Him.* See *Zohar* I:139a; 206b and 237a; III:171a.) For He is entirely unlimited by the confines of creation; the worlds do not effect any change in Him, heaven forbid, and He remains exactly the same as before creation.

This level cannot be attained by knowledge and intuition, for we cannot comprehend how creation makes no difference in Him. Rather, this is a concept of faith, "to *believe* in G-d"—that He, the Blessed One, is beyond the boundaries of worlds, and that before Him *darkness and light are equal.*[45] (See what is written in the discourse beginning *Vayar Yisroel...Vayaaminu BaHavaya.*[46])

3.

REINFORCING FAITH

Now, it is written: *Dwell in the land and nourish faith.*[47] To *nourish faith* means that one needs to reinforce it by "feeding" and nurturing, until the faith becomes ingrained in one's heart, so that one can connect with, relate to, and even visualize it.

Thus it will be in the time of Moshiach, as the verse says, *The earth will be filled with the knowledge [of G-d].*[48]

To explain: *Earth* refers to faith. Earth [is the lowest level of manifestation, and likewise, having faith] is the lowest aspect, where there is no revelation or explanation, just faith alone. We have the principle, "the beginning is wedged into

---

45. Psalms 139:12. Although one can fully relate to the fact that G-d created and sustains the universe, as explained in Chapter 1, nevertheless, the concept of G-d remaining *unchanged* by the creation of the universe is beyond our comprehension. And this is what we need to believe: that G-d "encompasses all worlds," and yet is unchanged by it.

46. *Torah Or, Beshalach* 62a: It is written (Exodus 14:31), *And they believed in G-d (Havaya).* This refers to the higher divine name (*Havaya Dil'eilah*) that is associated with the concealed worlds. It cannot be seen or understood and is only reached through faith.

47. Psalms 37:3. The literal meaning

כִּי וְלִגְדֻלָּתוֹ אֵין חֵקֶר כְּתִיב, וּכְתִיב אֶלֶף אֲלָפִים כו', וְעִנְיֵן בְּזֹהַר
חֵלֶק א' דַף רל"ט א'. וַיִּגַּשׁ דַּף ר"ו עַמּוּד ב', וַיְחִי דַּף רל"ז א'.
חֵלֶק ג' דַּף קע"א סוֹף עַמּוּד א') שֶׁאֵינוֹ בְּגֶדֶר עוֹלָמִין וְאֵין
הָעוֹלָמוֹת פּוֹעֲלִים בּוֹ שׁוּם שִׁנּוּי חַס וְשָׁלוֹם, וּכְמוֹ
מִקֹּדֶם שֶׁנִּבְרָא הָעוֹלָם.

וּבִבְחִינָה זוֹ לֹא שַׁיָּךְ דַּעַת וְהַרְגָּשָׁה, שֶׁאֵין נִתְפָּס
בְּשׁוּם שֵׂכֶל וְהַשָּׂגָה אֵיךְ אֵין שִׁנּוּי לְפָנָיו יִתְבָּרֵךְ, אֶלָּא זוֹ
הִיא בְּחִינַת אֱמוּנָה לְהַאֲמִין בָּהּ, שֶׁהוּא יִתְבָּרֵךְ אֵינוֹ בְּגֶדֶר
עוֹלָמִין וּלְפָנָיו כַּחֲשֵׁכָה כָּאוֹרָה (וְעִנְיַן מַה שֶּׁכָּתוּב מִזֶּה בִּדְרוּשׁ
הַמַּתְחִיל וַיַּרְא יִשְׂרָאֵל כו' וַיַּאֲמִינוּ בַּהוי'):

ג.

וְהִנֵּה כְּתִיב שְׁכָן אֶרֶץ וּרְעֵה אֱמוּנָה, פֵּרוּשׁ וּרְעֵה מְפַרְנֵס,
שֶׁצָּרִיךְ לְפַרְנֵס וּלְהַמְשִׁיךְ מָזוֹן לְהַגְדִּיל אֶת הָאֱמוּנָה, עַד
שֶׁתִּהְיֶה קְבוּעָה בְּלֵב הָאָדָם גַּם כֵּן בִּבְחִינַת דַּעַת וְהַרְגָּשָׁה,
וּכְאִלּוּ רוֹאֶה כו'.

וּכְמוֹ שֶׁיִּהְיֶה לֶעָתִיד לָבֹא, כְּדִכְתִיב וּמָלְאָה הָאָרֶץ
דֵּעָה.

פֵּרוּשׁ הָאָרֶץ, הִיא הָאֱמוּנָה שֶׁנִּקְרֵאת בְּשֵׁם אֶרֶץ,
שֶׁהִיא הַמַּדְרֵגָה הַתַּחְתּוֹנָה שֶׁאֵין בָּהּ גִּלּוּי אֶלָּא אֱמוּנָה

---

of this verse is that one's faith in G-d and resultant behavior sustains and nourishes the person (*Rashi*; *Metzudat David*). Chasidus interprets the verse as an instruction to actually nourish, or reinforce, faith—and the discourse proceeds to explain this. But first the discourse determines that this is at all possible, from the future time of Moshiach. For further reference, see sources cited below. p. 44.

48. Isaiah 11:9. The name of G-d in this verse is *Havaya*, which refers to the level of *sovev*, as explained below, in fn. 79. See also *Maamarei Admur HaEmtza'ee, Hanachot 5577*, p. 330.

the end":[49] the level of "beginning" is revealed only within that of "end" [i.e., the only way to bond with the greatest level, *sovev*, is through the simplest aspect—faith].[50]

[When Moshiach comes,] this faith will be *filled with knowledge*. It will be recognized and felt, as if we could see it, as is written, *the glory of G-d will be revealed, and all flesh together will see.*[51]

TORAH AND MITZVOT

The divine energy which causes the reinforcement of faith is stimulated through studying Torah and performing the *mitzvot*. (See what is written in the discourse beginning *Lehavin Inyan Haberachot*[52] and in *Iggeret Hakodesh*[53] on the verse, *She girds her loins with strength.*[54] See also the discourse *Ve'ehyeh Etzlo Amon*[55] and the discourse beginning *Moshe Yedaber*[56]

---

49. *Sefer Yetzirah* 1:7.

50. Even though we can only "grasp" the "beginning" and highest level, i.e., *sovev kol almin* through faith, it is nevertheless the "end" or simplest aspect of the person. The highest level is expressed in the simplest things. For example, when a person plans to build a house, the first thought which comes to mind is the general wish to have a house. Afterwards, however, when it comes to acting upon this wish, it is the opposite. First come the plans, followed by the gathering of the building materials, and finally, the construction. Similarly, the means with which to grasp the greatest level, *sovev*, is through the simplest aspect of the person, i.e., faith. (See R. DovBer of Mezritch, *Or Torah, Emor*.)

51. Isaiah 40:5. The fact that the flesh will see *the glory of G-d* will result from the nature and character of the flesh itself, just as our eyes, be-

cause of the way they are constructed, currently perceive physical things (*Likkutei Sichot*, vol. 17, p. 94).

52. *Torah Or, Bereishit* 6a: All Jews are believers sons of believers. Their faith is unattainable even by philosophers and thinkers since faith is beyond reason, transcending even the intellect of the G-dly soul, and "there is no thought which can grasp him." During the period of the first *Beit Hamikdash*, the souls of the Jewish people were in an exalted state. G-dliness rested and was revealed to them, causing their faith to be revealed as if actually seeing G-dliness. During the second *Beit Hamikdash* era, however, the souls were on a lower level. Therefore, the Men of the Great Assembly instituted the blessings to assist in eliciting and revealing this faith.

Here we have another case of "the divine energy which causes the reinforcement of faith"—here the recitation of blessings.

בְּלְבָךְ, כִּי נָעוּץ תְּחִלָּתָן בְּסוֹפָן, שֶׁאֵין גִּלּוּי תְּחִלָּתָן אֶלָּא
בִּבְחִינַת סוֹפָן.

וּבְחִינַת אֱמוּנָה זוֹ תִּהְיֶה מְלֵאָה דֵעָה, שֶׁתִּהְיֶה בִּבְחִינַת
הַכָּרָה וְהַרְגָּשָׁה, וּכְאִלּוּ רוֹאֶה וְכוּ'. וּכְמוֹ שֶׁכָּתוּב, וְנִגְלָה
כְּבוֹד ה' וְרָאוּ כָל בָּשָׂר יַחְדָּו כו'.

וְהַמְשָׁכָה זוֹ לִהְיוֹת הַגְדָּלַת הָאֱמוּנָה הוּא עַל
יְדֵי תּוֹרָה וּמִצְוֹת (וְעַיֵּן מַה שֶׁכָּתוּב בִּדְרוּשׁ הַמַּתְחִיל
לְהָבִין עִנְיַן הַבְּרָכוֹת, וּבְאִגֶּרֶת הַקֹּדֶשׁ עַל פָּסוּק חִגְרָה
בְעוֹז מָתְנֶיהָ. וְעַיֵּן מַה שֶׁכָּתוּב בִּדְרוּשׁ הַמַּתְחִיל וְאֶהְיֶה

---

53. Epistle 1: King Solomon said, *She girds her loins with strength.* The loins are the limbs that support the whole body, including the head positioned above them. These are the ones that bring the body to its desired destination.

Just as it is with the corporeality of the body, so it is with the spirituality of the soul. [The soul's loins] are the true belief in the One G-d…who permeates all worlds and encompasses all worlds…. This faith is referred to as the "loins" which uphold the "head," meaning the intellect that contemplates and concentrates on the greatness of G-d…. But what gives power to the loins to support and sustain the head and arms? It is one's involvement with, and study of, the laws of the Oral Torah…. This is the meaning of *She girds her loins with strength*: "there is no strength but Torah," for it gives power and strength to the loins, which are girded and embodied in it to strengthen and fortify its "arms." These, in turn, refer to the intellectually-generated and natural love and awe of G-d, in each man according to his measure.

54. Proverbs 31:17.

55. *Likkutei Torah, Bamidbar* 17d: One of the great qualities the Torah possesses is its ability to descend from its lofty state and act as a nurse who nurtures and nourishes the Jewish people. The Torah is therefore called the "food of the soul" as the verse states (Proverbs 9:5), *Come partake of my bread.*

56. *Torah Or, Yitro* 68b: Concerning Torah and *mitzvot* it is written, *Let us make man in our image and in our form.* "Image" refers to Torah and "form" to *mitzvot.* Together, they represent *the Man sitting on the likeness of the throne,* and express, in a revealed manner, the inner will and wisdom of G-d. The divine light within the Torah and *mitzvot* is neither concealed nor obscured; it is through them that G-d's infinite light is revealed below as it is above, so that *there is nothing besides Him.*

All of these references serve as proof-texts that Torah and *mitzvot* stimulate "the divine energy which causes the reinforcement of faith."

on the verse, *[Let us make man] in our image and in our likeness.*[57])

[We can attribute this reenforcement and stimulation of faith in the following way:

When creating man, G-d said:] *Let us make man* [Adam] *in our image, in our likeness.*[58] [The 248 limbs of man thus correspond to a similar G-dly level—] "the 248 G-dly limbs are the 248 [positive] *mitzvot.*"[59] [They are called "Supernal Man."[60]]

"*Adam*" has the same root as *edameh—I will be compared,*[61] [indicating that "Supernal Man"] is a reflection of an even higher level, i.e., the 248 forms of energy emanating from *sovev kol almin.*[62]

In general, the 248 *mitzvot* sub-divide into three categories: right, left, and center. These correspond to Torah study, *avodah*, and good deeds.[63]

TORAH

The words of Torah are the names of G-d.[64] Therefore when one reads the Torah, it is like calling G-d's name.[65]

GOOD DEEDS

"Good deeds" refers to the concept of charity, *to revive the*

---

57. Genesis 1:26.

58. Ibid. See *Rashi* there.

59. See *Tikkunei Zohar* 30 (74a).

60. Earthly man, *adam*, has been created in the image of *Adam Ha'elyon* (Supernal Man), referred to in the vision of Ezekiel (1:26).

61. Isaiah 14:14. Although the etymological origin of the word *adam* is *adamah*, earth (see *Bereishit Rabbah* 8:9), it may also be allusively derived from the verb *damah* ("compared"), from which also the word *demut* ("image") is derived. It is fittingly ex-

emplified in the aforementioned expression from Isaiah, ibid., as pointed out in the *Shaloh* 3a, 20b, 268b, 301b. See also *Asarah Maamarot, Maamar Eim Kol Chai*, part 2, ch. 33. See also above, fn. 14.

62. Just as there are 248 limbs in the body, each limb receiving a different type of energy from the soul according to its particular function, so, too, there are 248 G-dly "limbs," which are the 248 positive commandments—spiritual "vessels," collectively called *Adam Ha'elyon*. These vessels draw into them 248 different forms of energy from the level of *sovev*. Now, since *Adam Ha'elyon* itself is, af-

אֶצְלוֹ אָמוֹן, אָמוֹן פְּדְגוֹג. וּבְדְרוּשׁ הַמַּתְחִיל מֹשֶׁה וְדִבֶּר,
גַּבֵּי בְּצַלְמֵנוּ כִּדְמוּתֵנוּ),

שֶׁעֲלֵיהֶם נֶאֱמַר, נַעֲשֶׂה אָדָם בְּצַלְמֵנוּ כִּדְמוּתֵנוּ, רְמַ"ח
מִצְוֹת הֵם רְמַ"ח אֵבְרִין דְּמַלְכָּא –

בְּחִינַת אָדָם אֲדַמֶּה לְעֶלְיוֹן, שֶׁהֵם הֵן רְמַ"ח הַמְשָׁכוֹת
מִבְּחִינַת סוֹבֵב כָּל עָלְמִין.

וְדֶרֶךְ כְּלָל נֶחְלָקִין הָרְמַ"ח מִצְוֹת לְג' קַוִּין יָמִין וּשְׂמֹאל
וְאֶמְצָע, וְהֵם תּוֹרָה וַעֲבוֹדָה וּגְמִילוּת חֲסָדִים.

תּוֹרָה הוּא שְׁמוֹתָיו שֶׁל הַקָּדוֹשׁ בָּרוּךְ הוּא, קוֹרֵא
בַּתּוֹרָה הוּא כְּמוֹ שֶׁקּוֹרֵא בְּשֵׁם וְכוּ'.

וּגְמִילוּת חֲסָדִים זוֹ צְדָקָה, לְהַחֲיוֹת רוּחַ שְׁפָלִים עַל

---

ter all, also called "Adam" ("compared"), this indicates that it is "in the image of" something even higher, namely, *sovev kol almin*. Thus, by fulfilling Torah and *mitzvot*, one causes the lofty level of *sovev kol almin* to be drawn into *Adam Ha'elyon*, and in turn, to oneself, ultimately reinforcing one's belief in G-d. See *Maamarei Admur Hazaken 5566*, vol. 1, p. 396 ff.; *Or Hatorah, Devarim*, vol. 6, p. 2499.

63. See *Avot* 1:2. The ten G-dly attributes are placed into three categories: right, left and center. "Right" reflects the realm of kindness. "Left" reflects the realm of severity and justice. "Center" reflects the realm which harmonizes both the left and the right. The *mitzvot*, too, are divided into these categories: Kind deeds are on the right, *avodah* is on the left, and Torah study is in the

center. See *Bad Kodesh* p. 11, *Sefer Hamaamarim 5683*, p. 234.

The discourse will proceed to explain how each of these three categories of *mitzvot* cause the level of *sovev kol almin* to inspire the person who fulfills them.

64. *Zohar* II:87a; *Ramban*, introduction to his commentary on the Torah.

65. When one calls someone by name, it causes that person to come closer. Similarly, by studying Torah, G-d is called to come close, since the words of Torah are G-d's names. This is the meaning of the verse in Psalms (145:18), *G-d is close to all who call Him, to all who call Him in truth*, for "there is no 'truth' other than Torah" (Jerusalem Talmud, *Rosh Hashanah* 3:8). And, as a result, *sovev* is revealed. See *Tanya*, ch. 37.

spirit of the unfortunate.[66] This "awakening from below" triggers an "awakening from on High,"[67] which, in turn, causes a revelation from *sovev kol almin* to descend and *revive the unfortunate.*[68]

AVODAH

Avodah, the sacrificial offerings,[69] became earthly fire to be consumed in the heavenly fire.[70] So it is in prayer, which corresponds to the offerings;[71] the *Baruch She'amar* and the Verses of Praise[72] cause the "human fire" of G-dly love to intensify, and ascend on High.[73]

[Here are some selections from the Verses of Praise that stimulate love for G-d]:

"Blessed is the One who spoke, and the world came into being." That is, with "one statement" the world was created. Afterwards, this "one statement" was further clarified with nine sayings.[74]

Similarly, a subsequent paragraph says: *for His name is sublimely transcendent, it is unto Himself; only its radiance [is upon the earth and heavens]. He shall raise the glory of His people...the children of Israel, the people close to Him....*[75]

Likewise, other verses inspire and excite one's heart.

ROOTED AND INGRAINED

Now, *as water reflects a face back to a face,*[76] this motivation of

---

66. Isaiah 57:15.

67. The "awakening from below" is the inspiration of the soul which comes through one's effort to prevail over one's materialism and attempt to lift oneself up and draw closer to G-d. The "awakening from on High" refers to a spirit of holiness which descends to the person from above. Generally, to inspire this divine spirit, one needs to "awaken" it "from below," and this causes a heavenly response of similar nature. See *Zohar* I:77b, 86b, 88a; ibid.,

III:110b, 247b; *Iggeret Hakodesh* 4 and 5.

68. Not being exposed to G-dly revelation on a regular basis, the human being is considered "unfortunate." Although the energy of *sovev* is exalted and transcends creation, it descends to *revive the spirit of the unfortunate* as a result of a corresponding act of charity.

69. That *avodah* refers to the offerings, see for example, *Rashi, Rabbenu Yonah,* and *Bartenura* on *Avot* 1:2.

יְדֵי אִתְעָרוּתָא דִלְתַתָּא אִתְעָרוּתָא דִלְעֵלָּא, לִהְיוֹת הַמְשָׁכַת
סוֹבֵב כָּל עָלְמִין בִּבְחִינַת יְרִידָה וְהַשְׁפָּלָה לְהַחֲיוֹת רוּחַ
שְׁפָלִים.

וַעֲבוֹדָה זוֹ קָרְבָּנוֹת, בְּחִינַת רִשְׁפֵּי אֵשׁ שֶׁלְּמַטָּה לִכָּלֵל
בְּאֵשׁ שֶׁלְּמַעְלָה.

וְכֵן בִּתְפִלָּה שֶׁכְּנֶגֶד הַקָּרְבָּנוֹת תִּקְּנוּ, בָּרוּךְ שֶׁאָמַר וּפְסוּקֵי
דְזִמְרָה, לְהַגְדִּיל מְדוּרַת הָאֵשׁ הָאַהֲבָה שֶׁמִּמַּטָּה לְמַעְלָה –

בְּאָמְרוֹ בָּרוּךְ שֶׁאָמַר וְהָיָה הָעוֹלָם, דְּהַיְנוּ בְּמַאֲמָר
אֶחָד, וְאַחַר כָּךְ נִפְרָט עַל יְדֵי ט' מַאֲמָרוֹת כו'.

וְכֵן בְּהַלְלוּיָהּ, כִּי נִשְׂגָּב שְׁמוֹ לְבַדּוֹ רַק הוֹדוֹ גו' וַיָּרֶם
קֶרֶן לְעַמּוֹ וְגו' לִבְנֵי יִשְׂרָאֵל עַם קְרוֹבוֹ וְגו'.

וְכַיּוֹצֵא בָזֶה מִשְׁאָר פְּסוּקִים, שֶׁמֵּהֶם נִמְשָׁךְ רִשְׁפֵּי אֵשׁ
וְהִתְלַהֲטוּת הַלֵּב.

וְעַל יְדֵי זֶה כַּמַּיִם הַפָּנִים לַפָּנִים וְגו', מַמְשִׁיךְ לְמַטָּה

---

70. See *Yoma* 21b. In the *Beit Ha-mikdash*, the offerings were consumed by a fire upon the Altar. Although a heavenly fire would descend, it was a mitzvah to ignite a physical fire as well. Hence, the earthly fire was integrated into the heavenly fire.

71. See *Berachot* 26a-b (see also *Rabbenu Yonah* cited above).

72. Liturgy, Morning Prayer.

73. The section of the morning prayers from *Baruch She'amar* until *Yishtabach* is called "Verses of Praise." The discourse here explains that this section serves to intensify one's love of G-d, making this love ascend on High and integrating it with the heavenly fire.

74. See *Avot* 5:1; *Ramak, Pardes Rimonim* 2:6. See *Torat Shmuel—Sefer 5627*, p. 283.

75. Psalms 148:13-14. Although the entire creation is sustained through *memalei kol almin*, which is only a ray of *sovev kol almin*, the souls of the Jewish people derive from *sovev* itself. Thus, *He raises the glory of His people.* Meditating on this idea inspires a strong love for G-d. See *Maamarei Admur HaEmtza'ee, Hanachot 5577*, p. 257.

76. Proverbs 27:19.

the heart elicits a revelation from the realm of *sovev kol almin,* causing "faith" to become rooted and ingrained in one's heart and soul.[77]

IN THE LAND...

We can now explain the verses, *This is the commandment...to do in the land...a land flowing with milk and honey; Hear, O Israel, [the L-rd is our G-d, the L-rd is one].*

The meaning of the *Shema* chapter is:[78] *The Lord, sovev kol almin,* which is *our G-d,*[79] in Whom we believe by "pure faith"—should become *one*[80] throughout the seven heavens and earth,[81] in such a familiar and palpable manner [in Hebrew: *daat*] to the extent that it causes selfless devotion and true unity with G-d, to the point of reaching *yichuda ila'ah*[82]—an absolutely selfless devotion[83] (so is written in *Pri Eitz Chaim, Shaar Keriat Shema,* ch. 11, on the verse *the L-rd is One*—that this is the idea of eliciting the supernal *daat*).

---

77. Thus the discourse has presented examples of expressions of love for G-d, or "how the earthly fire integrates with the heavenly fire" during prayer.

78. The discourse proceeds to offer an esoteric explanation to the verse *Hear, O Israel, the Lord is our G-d, the Lord is one.*

79. In this verse, the Hebrew word for *the Lord* is *Havaya,* while the Hebrew word for *our G-d* is *Elokenu.*

HAVAYA / ELOKIM. *Havaya* and *Elokim* are two of the seven primary Divine names mentioned in Scripture. *Havaya* is the colloquial form—in Kabbalah and *Chakirah* (Torah philosophy)—of the Ineffable Divine Name, or Tetragrammaton, Y-H-V-H. The letters are rearranged so as not to pronounce the sacred Name.

Chasidus explains the difference between *Havaya* and *Elokim* thus: *Havaya* refers to the Infinite—transcending creation, nature, time and space completely—the level of Divinity that brings everything into existence *ex nihilo,* i.e., *sovev kol almin.* The name *Elokim* represents the level of G-d which conceals the Infinite Light and life-force, as this Infinite force is too intense for finite creatures to endure. *Elokim* is the power of G-d that makes the world appear as though it exists naturally and independently by itself, i.e., *memalei kol almin.* We see, for example, that the numerical value of *Elokim* is the same as the Hebrew word for "nature"—*hateva.*

80. See *Feminine Faith* (Kehot, 2009), ch. 3.

81. *Beit Yosef, Shulchan Aruch, Orach Chaim* 61:6.

בְּחִינַת סוֹבֵב כָּל עָלְמִין, שֶׁתִּהְיֶה אֱמוּנָה זוֹ קְבוּעָה וּתְקוּעָה
בְּלֵב וְנֶפֶשׁ הָאָדָם,

וְזֶהוּ וְזֹאת הַמִּצְוָה וְגוֹ' לַעֲשׂוֹת בָּאָרֶץ וְגוֹ' אֶרֶץ זָבַת
חָלָב וּדְבַשׁ שְׁמַע יִשְׂרָאֵל וְגוֹ'.

כִּי הִנֵּה עִנְיַן פָּרָשַׁת שְׁמַע יִשְׂרָאֵל הוּא, שֶׁהוּי' סוֹבֵב
כָּל עָלְמִין שֶׁהוּא אֱלֹהֵינוּ, שֶׁאֲנַחְנוּ מַאֲמִינִים בּוֹ בִּבְחִינַת
אֱמוּנָה לְבַדָּהּ, יִהְיֶה בִּבְחִינַת אֶחָד, בִּבְחִינַת גָּלוּי בְּשִׁבְעָה
רְקִיעִים וּבָאָרֶץ, בִּבְחִינַת דַּעַת וְהַרְגָּשָׁה (וְכֵן כָּתַב בִּפְרִי עֵץ
חַיִּים שַׁעַר הַקְּרִיאַת שְׁמַע פֶּרֶק י"א, בְּעִנְיַן הוי' אֶחָד, שֶׁהוּא הַמְשָׁכַת
הַדַּעַת עֶלְיוֹן כו') לִהְיוֹת בִּטּוּל וְיִחוּד אֲמִתִּי בִּבְחִינַת יְחוּדָא
עִלָּאָה, בִּטּוּל בִּמְצִיאוּת מַמָּשׁ.

The Talmud (*Berachot* 13b) states regarding the meditation on the word *echad* (one): "Once you acknowledge Him in your mind as King above and below and to the four corners—nothing more is required." This idea is hinted in the word *echad*: the *alef* (numerically equivalent to one) refers to G-d; the *chet* (numerically equivalent to eight) alludes to the seven heavens and the earth; the *dalet* (numerically equivalent to four) alludes to the four corners of the world. The word *echad*, then, can be understood to mean that although the seven heavens, the earth, and the four corners of the world were created, their existence does not contradict G-d's exclusivity because they are entirely nullified to the "*alef*," which is the Master of the world Who creates them (*True Existence* (Kehot, 2006), pp. 28-30).

Similar to the way the word *echad* implies that G-d is revealed throughout the seven heavens and the earth, personal faith, too, must penetrate

and be felt on a conscious level as well.

82. *Zohar* I:18b. *Yichuda ila'ah* is the Oneness of G-d from the perspective of *sovev*, as He completely transcends all worlds. The creation of the universe does not cause any change in G-d's Oneness. He remains the only being after the creation, just as He was before. When faith is internalized, one is able to rise and perceive the world from this perspective. See *Shaar Hayichud v'haEmunah*, ch. 7.

83. Hence, when the verse states, *Hear O Israel, the Lord is our G-d*, it refers to the level of G-dliness which transcends creation, and is unique to the Jewish people. At the same time, one is obligated to develop this faith so that it becomes felt on a conscious level. This is implied in the words "*the L-rd is one*" as explained in the previous footnote.

And this state of "reinforced" faith is achieved and realized by bringing the *mitzvot* to the level of "earth," i.e., to the level of faith [as indicated in the verse, *the commandments...in the land*].[84]

...FLOWING WITH MILK AND HONEY

Now, this "reinforced faith" is like *a land flowing with milk and honey*.

To explain: *Milk* refers to the developing of emotions,[85] implying that the love hidden in the heart intensifies and emerges from its dormant state. (The development of emotions results from one's faith that draws from the level of *sovev kol almin* specifically. For faith that draws from the level of *memalei kol almin* is unable to cause a love and fear of G-d beyond the capacity of one's soul. See what is written in the discourse beginning *Basi Legani* on the verse *I drank wine with milk*,[86] and in the discourse beginning *Chachlili Eiynayim*[87] on the verse *Rinsed in milk*,[88] and in the *Zohar* III:136b.)

Honey corresponds to sweetness and pleasure, as it is written: *Then you will delight in G-d.*[89]

This results from the level of *sovev kol almin*. That is, by meditating on the fact that although *I am G-d, I have not changed*, and "You [G-d] were the same before the world was created..." and *only its radiance is upon the earth*—nevertheless, *He shall raise the glory of His people...the children of Israel*, [for they are indeed] *the people close to Him*.[90]

With this meditation in mind one's heart becomes joyful and happy, and actually delights in G-dliness.

---

84. The fulfillment of *mitzvot* reinforces one's pre-existing natural faith. As explained above pp. 38-40, the fulfillment of *mitzvot* elicits energy from *sovev kol almin*, "causing one's faith to become rooted and ingrained in one's heart and soul."

This explanation resolves the third question of the discourse. *The land* mentioned in this verse does not refer to Israel, rather to *earth*, i.e., faith.

85. Milk causes growth. An infant develops far more while feeding on its mother's milk than it does when it grows older. In spiritual terms, "milk" refers to the reinforcement of the natural hidden love of G-d inherent in every Jew, thus causing this love to become revealed.

86. Song of Songs 5:1. *Likkutei Torah, Shir Hashirim* 32c: Just as milk is vital to a child's growth, and its consump-

וְנַעֲשָׂה וְנִמְשָׁךְ בְּחִינָה זוֹ עַל יְדֵי הַמְשָׁכַת הַמִּצְוֹת לִבְחִינַת אֶרֶץ, הִיא בְּחִינַת אֱמוּנָה.

וֶאֱמוּנָה זוֹ הִיא בְּחִינַת אֶרֶץ זָבַת חָלָב וּדְבַשׁ.

חָלָב הוּא בְּחִינַת הַגְדָּלַת הַמִדּוֹת, שֶׁתִּגְדַּל הָאַהֲבָה הַמְסֻתֶּרֶת בַּלֵּב וְתֵצֵא מֵהַהֶעְלֵם אֶל הַגִּלּוּי, (כִּי הַגְדָּלַת הַמִּדּוֹת הוּא עַל יְדֵי בְּחִינַת אֱמוּנָה מִבְּחִינַת סוֹבֵב כָּל עָלְמִין דַּיְקָא, מַה שֶׁאֵין כֵּן מִבְּחִינַת מְמַלֵּא כָּל עָלְמִין, לֹא תִּתְגַּדֵּל אַהֲבָתוֹ וְיִרְאָתוֹ לֵהּ' מִכַּאֲשֶׁר תּוּכַל נַפְשׁוֹ שְׂאֵת. וְעַיֵּן מַה שֶׁכָּתוּב בְּדְרוּשׁ הַמַּתְחִיל בָּאתִי לְגַנִּי, בְּפֵרוּשׁ יֵינִי עִם חֲלָבִי. וְסוֹף דְּרוּשׁ הַמַּתְחִיל חַכְלִילִי עֵינַיִם, גַּבֵּי רוֹחֲצוֹת בֶּחָלָב וּבַזֹּהַר חֵלֶק ג' קל"ו ב').

וּדְבַשׁ הוּא בְּחִינַת מְתִיקוּת וְתַעֲנוּג, כְּמוֹ שֶׁכָּתוּב אָז תִּתְעַנַּג עַל ה'.

וְהַיְנוּ מִבְּחִינַת סוֹבֵב כָּל עָלְמִין, דְּהַיְנוּ כַּאֲשֶׁר יִתְבּוֹנֵן כִּי אֲנִי הוי' לֹא שָׁנִיתִי, וְאַתָּה הוּא קֹדֶם שֶׁנִּבְרָא הָעוֹלָם כוּ'. וְרַק הוֹדוֹ עַל וְגוֹ'. וְעִם כָּל זֶה הִנֵּה וַיָּרֶם קֶרֶן לְעַמּוֹ וְלִבְנֵי יִשְׂרָאֵל עַם קְרוֹבוֹ מַמָּשׁ.

אֵי לָזֹאת יָגִיל וְיִשְׂמַח לִבּוֹ וְיִתְעַנַּג עַל ה' מַמָּשׁ.

---

tion enhances the development of the child's limbs, so does the revelation from *chochmah* develop the emotions of the soul—giving them an added infusion of divine light and a cleaving of the soul to the living G-d.

87. *Torah Or, Vayechi* 47d: The [spiritual counterpart of] milk rinses the emotions, transforming them from one form to another. It transforms the heart so that one is like an entirely new person with changed emotions

that are all equally positive.

88. Song of Songs 5:12.

89. Isaiah 58:14. Another effect of the faith becoming revealed is that the person enjoys great pleasure from this G-dly experience, as the discourse proceeds to explain. Hence the quote from Isaiah and the reference to honey.

90. See above, fn. 75.

LIVING THE GOOD LIFE

This explanation helps us understand the verse, *a righteous person lives by his faith.*[91] The term *lives* refers to "pleasure" and "invigoration."

[This meaning is also found in the following blessing:]

"[Blessed are You...] Creator of numerous living beings and their needs, for all the things You have created with which to sustain the soul of every living being."[92] [The first part of the blessing] "and their needs" refers to things which are necessary for a person's existence. [However, the second part,] "with which to sustain[93] the soul of every living being," refers to things which are only for pleasure and invigoration of the soul.[94]

In this vein, to *live by his faith* means that one is stimulated and feels elevated through faith more so than through any other pleasure and acquisition. As it says: *Whom [else] do I have in heaven? And with You, I do not desire [anything] on earth.*[95] (This, then, explains the verse [quoted at the opening of the chapter], *Nourish faith...and delight in the Lord*[96]—i.e. by *doing good.*[97] (See *Zohar* III:225b and 110b, and the commentary of *Ramaz* ad loc. *Zohar* II:170a, on the verse *A psalm by David, the Lord is my shepherd,*[98] and II:171a.))

4.

CHANGING TIMES

Yet, these attributes of milk and honey still do not reach the state when *the earth will be filled with knowledge of G-d,*[48] referring to the time of Moshiach when this knowledge will be tangibly experienced. Presently, however, the attributes of milk and honey are still in the realm of faith.[99]

---

91. Habakkuk 2:4.

92. Liturgy, Blessing After Other Foods and Drink.

93. I.e., "upkeep," "bolster," "reinforce."

94. *Tur* and *Beit Yosef, Orach Chaim,* 207.

Man's requirements can be divided into two categories. In order to exist, the bare necessities are sufficient. However, to "live" and thrive, one needs to have enthusiasm and enjoyment. In terms of the faith discussed here, the first category refers to revealing the love inherently hidden in the heart, while the second category

וְזֶהוּ וְצַדִּיק בֶּאֱמוּנָתוֹ יִחְיֶה, מִלְּשׁוֹן תַּעֲנוּג וּפִקּוּחַ נֶפֶשׁ.

כְּמוֹ בּוֹרֵא נְפָשׁוֹת רַבּוֹת וְחֶסְרוֹנָם עַל כָּל מַה שֶׁבָּרֵאתָ לְהַחֲיוֹת בָּהֶם נֶפֶשׁ כָּל חַי, שֶׁפֵּרוּשׁ חֶסְרוֹנָם, דָּבָר הֶחָסֵר לָאָדָם לְקִיּוּם חַיּוּתוֹ, לְהַחֲיוֹת בָּהֶם נֶפֶשׁ כָּל חַי, שֶׁאֵינוֹ אֶלָּא לְהִתְעַנֵּג וּפִקּוּחַ נֶפֶשׁ.

וְכָךְ יִחְיֶה בֶּאֱמוּנָתוֹ, לְהָשִׁיב אֶת נַפְשׁוֹ יוֹתֵר מִכָּל הַתַּעֲנוּגִים וּמֵרֹב כָּל, וּכְמוֹ שֶׁכָּתוּב מִי לִי בַשָּׁמָיִם וְעִמְּךָ לֹא חָפַצְתִּי וְגו'. (וְזֶהוּ וּרְעֵה אֱמוּנָה וְהִתְעַנֵּג עַל ה', וְהַיְנוּ עַל יְדֵי וַעֲשֵׂה טוֹב. (וְעַיֵּן זֹהַר חֵלֶק ג' פִּינְחָס דַּף רכ"ה ב' מֵעִנְיָן זֶה. וּבְפָרָשַׁת בְּהַר דַּף ק"י עַמּוּד ב'. וּבְפֵרוּשׁ הָרַמַ"ז שָׁם מֵעִנְיָן טוֹב. חֵלֶק ב' תְּרוּמָה ק"ע עַמּוּד א' עַל פָּסוּק מִזְמוֹר לְדָוִד ה' רֹעִי, וְדַף קע"א א'))׃

ד.

אַךְ בְּחִינוֹת אֵלּוּ שֶׁל חָלָב וּדְבַשׁ, עֲדַיִן לֹא הִגִּיעוּ לְמַעֲלַת וּמַדְרֵגַת וּמָלְאָה הָאָרֶץ דֵּעָה שֶׁיִּהְיֶה לֶעָתִיד לָבֹא בְּחִינַת דַּעַת וְהַרְגָּשָׁה מַמָּשׁ, מַה שֶּׁאֵין כֵּן חָלָב וּדְבַשׁ הֵם בְּחִינַת הָאֱמוּנָה עֲדַיִן.

---

refers to the enjoyment of this revelation, which constantly invigorates and inspires a righteous person.

95. Psalms 73:25.
To summarize: The objective is that one's faith become like milk and honey, growing and developing as one lives and experiences pleasure. This growth is accomplished through fulfilling the Torah and *mitzvot*, as explained earlier.

96. Psalms 37:3-4. Literally, the verses read: *Trust in the Lord and do good; then you will abide in the land and be nourished by faith. Delight in the Lord, and He will grant you the desires of your heart."* And the Chasidic translation

offered here is: *Do good* refers to the study of Torah and performance of *mitzvot*, which "nourishes faith," i.e., reinforcing and strengthening the belief in G-d, enabling one to *delight in the Lord.* See above, fn. 47.

97. Ibid., 37:3.

98. Ibid., 23:1.

99. Nowadays, although one might toil to internalize faith, as described above, it still remains somewhat remote and abstract. When Moshiach comes, however, the knowledge of *Havaya* will *fill the earth*, so that one will be able fully to relate to it on a personal level.

It is quite apparent that the world, in its routine func-
tioning, receives its energy from the level of *memalei kol almin*, which is why there's a set time for everything. For in-
stance, the snake infused an impurity in Eve.[100] [Eve] refers to
Knesset Yisrael.[101] At the Giving of the Torah, this impurity
ceased.[102] Later on, with the sin of the golden calf, it re-
turned.[103] Subsequently, in Joshua's time people served G-d,
but in the era of the Judges they did not. In the days of David
and Solomon they were at a very elevated level, while afterwards, with the sin of Jeroboam [they fell].[104] So it is in every generation, changes occur according to the circumstances.
In the times of the Tannaim and Amoraim[105] as well, one period was not similar to the next. In all eras there is change and
transformation.

These changes occur because events are governed by the
level of *memalei kol almin*. This level is likened to a figure
with a head, hands, feet, and other limbs; each limb is different from the other, with diverse functions. Furthermore,
sometimes, one of the limbs is in pain or weakened, as well as
other changing conditions that can occur. (See *Zohar* I:221a;
III:107; III:281a. See also Pardes, *Shaar Ab'ya*, ch. 1)

Changes also happen to a person as well. At times one
transgresses with a forbidden thought, speech, or action, and
at other times, one has thoughts of repentance and good
deeds. *Everything has its time...,*[106] *And the might shall pass
from one regime to the other*[107]—that is, when one rises the
other falls. "Tyre would not have flourished [if not for the destruction of Jerusalem]."[108]

---

100. See Genesis 3.

101. See *Shaar Maamarei Rashbi*, p. 193.
    KNESSET YISRAEL (Community of Israel), in a spiritual sense refers to the source from which the individual souls descend and are sustained, at times identified with the *Shechinah* (Divine Presence) itself.

102. *Shabbat* 146a.

103. See Exodus 32; *Zohar* I:52b; II:193b.

104. These different eras are de-scribed in the Books of Joshua, Judg-es, Samuel, and Kings.

105. TANNAIM: The sages of the

וְהָעִנְיָן, כִּי הִנֵּה אָנוּ רוֹאִים שֶׁהָעוֹלָם כְּמִנְהָגוֹ נוֹהֵג,
בִּבְחִינַת מְמַלֵּא כָּל עָלְמִין, שֶׁיֵּשׁ לְכָל עֵת כו'. כִּי הַנָּחָשׁ
הִטִּיל זוּהֲמָא בְּחַוָּה, בְּחִינַת כְּנֶסֶת יִשְׂרָאֵל, וּבְמַתַּן תּוֹרָה
פָּסְקָה זוּהֲמָתָן. וְאַחַר כָּךְ בְּחֵטְא הָעֵגֶל חָזַר כו'. וְאַחַר כָּךְ
בִּימֵי יְהוֹשֻׁעַ עָבְדוּ אֶת ה', וּבִימֵי שְׁפוֹט הַשּׁוֹפְטִים קִלְקְלוּ,
וּבִימֵי דָוִד וּשְׁלֹמֹה הָיוּ בְּמַעֲלָה הָעֶלְיוֹנָה, וְאַחַר כָּךְ
בְּחֵטְא יָרָבְעָם כו', וְכָךְ בְּכָל דּוֹר וָדוֹר נִשְׁתַּנָּה לְפִי הָעִנְיָן,
וְגַם בִּימֵי הַתַּנָּאִים וְהָאֲמוֹרָאִים אֵין זְמַן אֶחָד דּוֹמֶה לַחֲבֵרוֹ,
וְכָל הָעִתִּים מִשְׁתַּנִּים, וְהַזְּמַנִּים מִתְחַלְּפִין וּמִתְהַפְּכִין.

וְהַיְינוּ לְפִי שֶׁהֵם בִּבְחִינַת מְמַלֵּא כָּל עָלְמִין, שֶׁהֵם
בְּחִינַת פַּרְצוּף רֹאשׁ וְיָד וְרֶגֶל וּשְׁאָר אֵבָרִים, שֶׁאֵין אֶחָד
דּוֹמֶה לַחֲבֵרוֹ, וּפְעֻלַּת הָאֵיבָרִים מִשְׁתַּנִּין, גַּם לִפְעָמִים
כּוֹאֵב אֶחָד מֵהָאֵבָרִים אוֹ נֶחֱלָשׁ כו', וְכַיּוֹצֵא בָּזֶה שִׁנּוּיִם
מִקְרִים (וְעַיֵּן זֹהַר חֵלֶק א' וַיְחִי דַף רכ"א א' דְּאִשְׁתַּנִּיאַת מִגַּוְנָא
לְגַוְנָא, וְסוֹף פָּרָשַׁת אֱמוֹר דַּף ק"ז. זֹהַר חֵלֶק ג' תֵּצֵא רפ"א א', וְעַיֵּן
בְּפַרְדֵּס שַׁעַר אבי"ע סוֹף פֶּרֶק א').

וְכֵן בְּכָל אָדָם בִּפְרָטִיּוּת, לִפְעָמִים נוֹפֵל בְּמַחֲשָׁבָה
דִּבּוּר וּמַעֲשֶׂה אֲשֶׁר לֹא טוֹב. וְלִפְעָמִים יִפּוֹל לוֹ הִרְהוּרֵי
תְּשׁוּבָה וּמַעֲשִׂים טוֹבִים, כִּי לְכָל עֵת וְגו' וּלְאֹם מִלְאֹם
יֶאֱמָץ. כְּשֶׁזֶּה קָם כו'. לֹא נִתְמַלְאָה צוֹר כו'.

Mishnah who lived between the era of the Men of the Great Assembly and Rabbi Yehudah Hanassi (C. 350 BCE to 150 CE).

AMORAIM: The sages of the Talmud who lived following the Tannaim until the completion of the Talmud (C. 150-500 CE).

106. See Ecclesiastes 3:1.

107. Genesis 25:23. Holiness and evil are likened to two regimes waging war over a city. When one is more powerful, the other is weakened. At times, the side of holiness is stronger, leaving the evil side weakened, and vice versa. See *Tanya*, ch. 9.

108. *Rashi* on Genesis, ibid. See *Megillah* 6a.

Therefore, a person should not despair when seeing himself fall, since this is the nature of the changing times, and one can later return and transform his negative energy into something positive.

This all is an expression of the level of *memalei kol almin*.

ERADICATION OF EVIL

However, in order for the level of *sovev kol almin* to be revealed in a recognizable way, *You shall abolish evil...* [109] (as elucidated in the explanatory addendum to the discourse, *Ki Al Kol Kavod Chuppah* [110]). This state will be in the future days, when the prophecy *I will remove the spirit of impurity from the land* [111] will be fulfilled.

EVIL AT WORK

This was not the case, however, at the time of the destruction of the *Beit Hamikdash* [112]: At the time of the first *Beit Hamikdash* there were false prophets, [113] and at the second *Beit Hamikdash*, the people displayed baseless hatred toward each other. [114] These were the "opposites" of faith that transcends reason.

To explain: Just as in the side of holiness there is the level of faith which transcends reason, on the other side, too, there were false beliefs amongst the Jewish people (as described in Jeremiah 44:17-18).

---

109. Deuteronomy 13:6.

110. *Likkutei Torah, Shir Hashirim* 48a: It is stated that in future times we will be given a "new Torah"... containing the hidden reasons for the *mitzvot*. This is a revelation of *mochin stima'ah* (concealed intellect) and [a revelation of] the delight contained within the divine will. Currently, this level is hidden, but in the future it will be revealed and we will delight with the L-rd....

The reason that this revelation will only occur in future times is as follows:

The purpose of the *mitzvot* is to refine and elevate the divine sparks by performing positive commandments, and isolating what is evil by abstaining from transgression of the negative commandments. For everything, even a Jewish soul, contains positive and negative elements because, when the 248 divine sparks fell into this world, they became mixed together with negative elements. By performing the *mitzvot*, these divine sparks become separated and refined, and rise to a higher level....

Currently—prior to the comple-

וְעַל כֵּן, אַל יִפּוֹל לֵב הָאָדָם עָלָיו בִּרְאוֹתוֹ שֶׁנּוֹפֵל
כוּ', כִּי כָּךְ הוּא סֵדֶר תַּהְפּוּכוֹת הַזְּמַן, וְיָכוֹל הוּא לַחֲזוֹר
וּלְשַׁנּוֹת אֶת טַעֲמוֹ מֵרַע לְטוֹב.

וְכָל זֶה הוּא בִּבְחִינַת מְמַלֵּא כָּל עָלְמִין.

אַךְ לִהְיוֹת בְּחִינַת סוֹבֵב כָּל עָלְמִין בִּבְחִינַת גִּלּוּי,
בִּבְחִינַת דַּעַת וְהַרְגָּשָׁה מַמָּשׁ, צָרִיךְ לִהְיוֹת וּבִעַרְתָּ הָרָע וְגו'
(וּכְמוֹ שֶׁכָּתוּב מִזֶּה בַּבֵּאוּר עַל פָּסוּק כִּי עַל כָּל כָּבוֹד חֻפָּה) שֶׁזֶּה
יִהְיֶה לֶעָתִיד לָבֹא, שֶׁיָּקִים וְאֶת רוּחַ הַטֻּמְאָה אַעֲבִיר מִן הָאָרֶץ.

מַה שֶּׁאֵין כֵּן בִּזְמַן חֻרְבַּן הַבַּיִת, שֶׁבַּיִת רִאשׁוֹן הָיוּ בּוֹ
נְבִיאֵי הַשֶּׁקֶר, וּבַיִת שֵׁנִי הָיָה בּוֹ שִׂנְאַת חִנָּם, שֶׁהֵם הֵם
בְּחִינַת זֶה לְעֻמַּת זֶה, כְּנֶגֶד בְּחִינַת אֱמוּנָה שֶׁהִיא לְמַעְלָה מִן
הַדַּעַת,

וְהָעִנְיָן, כִּי כְּמוֹ שֶׁיֵּשׁ בְּסִטְרָא דִקְדֻשָּׁה בְּחִינַת אֱמוּנָה
שֶׁהִיא לְמַעְלָה מִן הַדַּעַת, כָּךְ הָיָה אָז בֵּין יִשְׂרָאֵל אֱמוּנוֹת
כּוֹזְבוֹת (כִּמְבֹאָר בְּיִרְמְיָהוּ סִמָּן מ"ד פָּסוּק י"ז י"ח).

---

tion of the refinement process—this level of delight cannot be revealed, since good and evil are still combined together. Only when the divine sparks have been refined and elevated to their former [higher] state—completing the objective of creation—and evil no longer conceals the good, can the pleasure from the supernal light be revealed.

Hence, by abolishing evil, through the process of refinement, "the level of *sovev kol almin* will be revealed."

111. Zechariah 13:2. The level of *sovev* negates entirely any other entity aside from G-dliness (see above, fn. 79). Therefore, so long as there is any negativity in the world, *sovev* cannot

be fully revealed. When Moshiach comes, the energy of *sovev* will *fill the earth* and will be felt and experienced by all because the impure spirit will be removed, as the discourse continues.

112. The greatest time of G-dly revelation for the Jewish people so far was when the *Beit Hamikdash* stood (see *Sefer Hamaamarim Melukat*, vol. 3, pp. 190 & 193). Yet, even then it wasn't possible to internalize this faith in a discernable way, due to the prevalent evil at the time.

113. See below.

114. See *Yoma* 9b.

At the time of the first *Beit Hamikdash*, the forces of holiness were clearly evident, with the Divine Presence revealed along with the Holy Ark and its cover [in place].[115] Conversely, as the forces of *kelipah* grew powerful because of the sins, there was an increase in the forces denying the belief in G-d. [This resulted in idol worship. For example,] the women would cause the Tammuz idol to cry.[116] They also said: *Ever since we stopped burning incense to the queen of the heavens...we have lacked everything.*[117] There were also false prophets (as stated in Jeremiah 27:14, 15) who corrupted the people's beliefs, leading them to believe things that G-d had never said.

At the time of the second *Beit Hamikdash*, however, five key elements present in the first one were missing.[118] Therefore, also on the opposing side the forces of *kelipah* were not as powerful. So the negative beliefs concerned worldly matters, such as believing tale-bearers which caused hatred between people. This hatred was baseless, for indeed one's fellow did not do him any harm. If the tale-bearers would not have been believed, there would definitely not have been hatred toward one's fellow man, for it is unnatural to hate one's friend for no reason, knowing that indeed his friend did him no wrong.

5.

IN THE VERSES

We can now explain the verse, *Today, you should know and take to your heart....*

Concerning knowledge and sensation of the level of *memalei kol almin*, the verse already says, *You have been*

---

115. The Ark was the holiest part of the *Beit Hamikdash* since the Divine Presence rested upon it. But this was the case only in the first *Beit Hamikdash*, for in the second *Beit Hamikdash* the Ark was not in its proper place in the Holy of Holies but buried underneath the *Beit Hamikdash*. See *Horiyot* 12a and *Yoma* 52b; *Rambam, Hilchot Beit Habechirah* 4:1.

116. See Ezekiel 8:14. The Tammuz was an idol with eyes of lead. When

וְהֵם זֶה לְעֻמַּת זֶה, וְהִנֵּה בְּבַיִת רִאשׁוֹן בְּהִתְגַּבְּרוּת סִטְרָא דִקְדֻשָּׁה הָיָה גִּלּוּי שְׁכִינָה אָרוֹן וְכַפֹּרֶת, וְכָךְ בְּזֶה לְעֻמַּת זֶה, בְּהִתְגַּבְּרוּת סִטְרָא דִקְלִפָּה מֵחֲמַת הַחֵטְא הָיָה הִתְגַּבְּרוּת כְּנֶגֶד אֱמוּנַת אֱלֹהוּת, וְהַנָּשִׁים שֶׁהָיוּ מְבַכּוֹת אֶת הַתַּמּוּז אָמְרוּ מֵעֵת חָדַלְנוּ לְקַטֵּר לִמְלֶכֶת שָׁמַיִם חָסַרְנוּ וְגוֹ', וְכָךְ הָיוּ נְבִיאֵי הַשֶּׁקֶר (כְּמוֹ שֶׁכָּתוּב בְּיִרְמְיָה סִמָּן כ"ז פָּסוּק י"ד ט"ז), דְּהַיְנוּ אֱמוּנוֹת כּוֹזְבוֹת בְּנָבִיא, לְהַאֲמִין בְּמַה שֶּׁלֹּא דִבֶּר ה',

מַה שֶּׁאֵין כֵּן בְּבַיִת שֵׁנִי, שֶׁחָסְרוּ ה' דְּבָרִים לֹא הָיְתָה גַּם כֵּן בִּלְעֻמַּת זֶה הִתְגַּבְּרוּת הַקְּלִפָּה כָּל כָּךְ, וְהָיְתָה הָאֱמוּנָה רָעָה בְּמִלֵּי דְעָלְמָא, לְהַאֲמִין בְּאַנְשֵׁי רָכִיל לִשְׂנֹוא אֶת חֲבֵרוֹ, שֶׁהַשִּׂנְאָה הַהִיא הִיא שִׂנְאַת חִנָּם, שֶׁחֲבֵרוֹ לֹא עָשָׂה לוֹ רָעָה בֶּאֱמֶת. כִּי אִם לֹא הָיָה מַאֲמִין בְּאַנְשֵׁי רָכִיל, בְּוַדַּאי לֹא הָיָה אִישׁ שׂוֹנֵא לְרֵעֵהוּ כְּלָל, שֶׁזֶּה כְּנֶגֶד הַטֶּבַע שֶׁיִּשְׂנָא אֶחָד לַחֲבֵרוֹ חִנָּם אִם יוֹדֵעַ בֶּאֱמֶת שֶׁחֲבֵרוֹ לֹא פָּשַׁע כוּ':

ה.

וְזֶהוּ וְיָדַעְתָּ הַיּוֹם וַהֲשֵׁבֹתָ אֶל לְבָבֶךָ וְגוֹ',

כִּי לִהְיוֹת הַיְדִיעָה וְהָרְגָּשָׁה בִּבְחִינַת מְמַלֵּא כָּל עָלְמִין,

---

heated up from the inside, these eyes would melt, creating the illusion that the idol was crying and begging for offerings (*Rashi*).

117. See Jeremiah 44:18. The queen of the heavens was another object of idolatry.

118. See *Yoma* 21b: "Five elements were [lacking and thus made a difference] between the first and second *Batei Mikdash*, as follows: the Ark with its cover and *keruvim*, the fire, the Divine Presence, the divine spirit, and the oracle parchment of the *kohen gadol's* breastplate." This caused a diminished holiness, which resulted in a much weaker opposition from the other side.

shown..., in the past tense.[119] However, the verse, *Today, you should know* refers to knowledge at the level of *sovev kol almin.*

[Thus the verse continues]: *In the heaven above—the heaven* refers to *sovev.* For just as the heavens are spherical and the earth is in the center surrounded by the heavens (see what is written in the discourse *Ki Hamitzvah Hazot*[120] on the verse *It is not in the heavens*[121]) likewise, the spoken word of G-d, *memalei kol almin,* is encompassed by *sovev kol almin,* for "there is nothing external to G-d."[122] We might compare this to words which remain within us before they are spoken.[123]

PRESENT WORLD VS. THE WORLD TO COME

This level can be experienced *today,* specifically[124] [as opposed to after one's lifetime]. As it says regarding the *mitzvot: today, they are to be done,*[125] not tomorrow, in the World to Come.[126]

The World to Come is sustained by the level of *memalei kol almin* [—where] levels progress from point to point, stage after stage. By way of analogy, just as a figure has a head, hands, and feet, so there are many sub-levels in *me-*

---

119. At the Giving of the Torah the people were shown that G-d is the Creator and rules over the world. See above, fn. 2. This is the concept of *memalei kol almin* (fn. 22).

120. *Likkutei Torah, Nitzavim* 45d: Scripture states: *[The Torah] is neither in the heavens nor across the sea.* "Heaven" refers to the heavenly light surrounding everything which is not visible from earth. Even the bluish color that we see is only a result of reflections in the atmosphere and not the true image of the heavens.

This reference is cited as proof-text that the heavens encompass the earth.

121. Deuteronomy 30:12.

122. *Tanya,* ch. 21.

123. The soul has potential to perform a variety of tasks, such as thinking and feeling. The capability to express one's thoughts to others through speech is one of the many features and components in the person's makeup. However, once a person actually exercises his power of speech to produce a specific word, that word has become separate from his soul, and is now an independent entity that can be heard by a stranger. G-d, too, has the ability to limit

כְּבָר נֶאֱמַר אַתָּה הָרְאֵתָ לָדַעַת וְגוֹ'. כְּבָר הָרְאֵתָ כוּ'. אֲבָל לִהְיוֹת וְיָדַעְתָּ בִּבְחִינַת סוֹבֵב כָּל עָלְמִין –

דְּהַיְנוּ בַּשָּׁמַיִם מִמַּעַל, שָׁמַיִם בְּחִינַת סוֹבֵב, כְּמוֹ הַשָּׁמַיִם שֶׁהֵם כַּדּוּרִים וּכְמוֹ הָאָרֶץ שֶׁהִיא בְּתוֹךְ הַשָּׁמַיִם וְהַשָּׁמַיִם מַקִּיפִין לָהּ (וְעִנְיַן מַה שֶּׁכָּתוּב בִּדְרוּשׁ הַמַּתְחִיל כִּי הַמִּצְוָה הַזֹּאת גַּבֵּי לֹא בַשָּׁמַיִם הִיא). כָּךְ הִנֵּה דְבַר ה', הוּא בְּחִינַת מְמַלֵּא כָּל עָלְמִין, הִיא מְקֶפֶת בִּבְחִינַת סוֹבֵב כָּל עָלְמִין, שֶׁאֵין דָּבָר חוּץ מִמֶּנּוּ. וּכְמָשָׁל הַדִּבּוּר בְּעוֹדוֹ בְּכֹחַ הַנֶּפֶשׁ, שֶׁעֲדַיִן לֹא יָצָא וְנִפְרַד כוּ'.

וִידִיעָה זֶהוּ הוּא דַּוְקָא הַיּוֹם, כְּמוֹ הַיּוֹם לַעֲשׂוֹתָם וְלֹא לְמָחָר בָּעוֹלָם הַבָּא,

שֶׁהָעוֹלָם הַבָּא הוּא בְּחִינַת מְמַלֵּא כָּל עָלְמִין, הִשְׁתַּלְשְׁלוּת הַמַּדְרֵגוֹת מֵעֲלָה לְעָלוּל מַדְרֵגָה אַחַר מַדְרֵגָה,

---

and contract His infinite energy of *sovev* to produce the contained energy of *memalei* which sustains creation. However, this energy remains concealed within creation, rather than revealing itself as a "spreading forth" of G-d's infinite light. Yet, this "power of limitation" is merely a part of G-d's infinite capacity and all-inclusiveness. Now, although the universe was created, from G-d's perspective, the universe is viewed as in its "potential" state, i.e., G-d's power of limitation, rather than it being an independent entity. For there can be no form of existence external to G-d Himself (see above, fn. 79). To man, however, the world seems to be an independent entity, similar to that of a spoken word. See *Tanya*, ch. 21;

Shaar Hayichud v'haEmunah, chs. 3-4.

The opening question of the discourse is now resolved. The verse *You have been shown* refers to the revelation of *memalei kol almin*. The verse *Today you should know*, however, is the commandment to meditate on and internalize the level of *sovev kol almin*.

124. Here begins the answer to the second question of the discourse.

125. Deuteronomy 7:11.

126. See *Avodah Zara* 4b. Here referring to the World to Come after passing from life on earth and not the world in the times of Moshiach.

malei kol almin: Higher Gan Eden, Lower Gan Eden, and so on.[127]

Therefore, a person's forbidden thoughts, speech, and deeds become "soiled garments" worn by his soul in the World to Come. He cannot remove these garments himself, and it is like being tied in a sack. Only through *kaf hakela*[128] and similar processes can these restraints be loosened and untied[129] (as explained in the discourse beginning *Tzav Et Bnei Yisroel*[130]).

Today, in this world, however, it is different. One has the chance to *take to heart* (in the plural), referring to both inclinations,[131] through implementing *itkafia* and *it'hapcha*.[132] *Today* it is possible to refine and transform evil by wey of *sovev kol almin*.

---

127. GAN EDEN. There are two levels of Gan Eden, known as "higher" and "lower" Gan Eden. See *Tanya*, Bi-Lingual Edition, p. 601, note 10, for a discussion on "Higher and Lower Gan Eden."

(These correspond to *Beriah* and *Asiyah* respectively and also to *binah* and *malchut* of *Atzilut*. See *Zohar* III:128b in *Idra Rabbah*; *Sefer Halikkutim, Gan Eden*, chapter 2; *Sefer Hamaamarim Melukat*, vol. 2, p. 229—and sources cited there.)

128. KAF HAKELA. The "hollow of a sling." See I Samuel 25:29—*And he shall fling away the souls of your enemies, as out of the hollow of a sling*. Eschatologically interpreted in *Shabbat* 152b as the means for cleansing the souls of the wicked in the afterlife, the soul is shot back and forth by the angels to re-experience the physical world. It is shown a replay of its careless thoughts, speech, and actions, which causes great pain and regret to the soul. See also *Likkutei Torah, Pinchas* 75c.

129. Both this world and the world of the afterlife are similar in the sense that they are sustained through *memalei kol almin*. Yet, this world has the potential to bring forth the level of *sovev* as well, because in this world the holy and evil forces are mixed together. Man's purpose is to refine the evil and transform it into the holy, which can be accomplished through the energy of *sovev* alone—brought down to the world through Torah study and mitzvah performance. Only this limitless energy can entirely transform the evil into something holy. The afterlife, however, is a completely new phase, where each level exists on its own. The holy and evil are no longer intermingled and the focus of transforming evil exists no longer. So if the soul enters the afterlife with "soiled garments" caked to it, it must endure the cleansing process in order to progress. Moreover, since the evil can no longer be transformed, the option of eliciting *sovev* is not available.

130. *Likkutei Torah, Pinchas* 75b-c:

וּכְמָשָׁל פַּרְצוּף שֶׁיֵּשׁ בּוֹ רֹאשׁ וְיָד וְרֶגֶל כו'. כָּךְ יֵשׁ מַדְרֵגוֹת
רַבּוֹת גַּן עֵדֶן עֶלְיוֹן וְגַן עֵדֶן תַּחְתּוֹן כו'.

וְלָכֵן הַמַּעֲשִׂים וְדִבּוּרִים וּמַחֲשָׁבוֹת נַעֲשׂוּ לְבוּשִׁין
צוֹאִים לָעוֹלָם הַבָּא, וְאֵין יָכוֹל לִפְשׁוֹט אוֹתָם, וּכְאִלּוּ
קָשׁוּר בְּשַׂק, אִם לֹא עַל יְדֵי כַּף הַקֶּלַע וְכַיּוֹצֵא בָזֶה,
לְהַתִּיר וּלְהַפְקִיעַ הַקֶּשֶׁר וְכו' (וּכְמוֹ שֶׁנִּתְבָּאֵר בִּדְרוּשׁ הַמַּתְחִיל
צַו אֶת בְּנֵי יִשְׂרָאֵל כו' אֶת קָרְבָּנִי לַחְמִי),

מַה שֶּׁאֵין כֵּן הַיּוֹם, וַהֲשֵׁבֹתָ אֶל לְבָבֶךָ, בִּשְׁנֵי יְצָרֶיךָ,
בִּבְחִינַת אִתְכַּפְיָא וְאִתְהַפְכָא כו', שֶׁהַיּוֹם יָכוֹל לְבָרֵר
וּלְהַפְרִיד הָרָע עַל יְדֵי הַמְשָׁכָה מִבְּחִינַת סוֹבֵב כָּל עָלְמִין –

This world is a place of action in which we are given the ability to choose good. Even if one has transgressed, there is still the opportunity to repent and return to G-d. In the World to Come, however, this freedom of choice is not provided; the way one lived in this world is the way it remains in the World to Come.

And despite the great revelation of G-dliness which exists in the World to Come—to the extent that all beings exist in a state of subservience to G-d, and even the negative forces recognize that G-d is the ultimate King—man is nevertheless unable to take control and free himself from the imprisonment of the body and from the forces of the animal soul, pursued while in this world.

This is the concept of *kaf hakela*: The individual is thrown back to re-experience the worthless thoughts he pursued while in this world.... A person's thoughts, speech, and action—which act as the garments of the soul—become like sackcloth and soiled apparel in the World to Come.

The soul is dressed from head to toe in these garments and is unable to free itself from them. It is only through the purification process of *kaf hakela* that they can be removed.

131. I.e., the good and the evil, see *Berachot* 54a.

132. ITKAFIA and IT'HAPCHA. These are two parts of the "refining system," which purify the animal soul and direct it towards the service of G-d. In *itkafia*, the animal soul still has the urge to indulge in selfish and evil things, but the person subdues, i.e., controls and disciplines, those selfish impulses. In the second part of the "refining system," which occurs as a result of the first, the person is able to master the impulses of the animal soul and not succumb to doing or even thinking evil—and then reaches *it'hapcha* (lit., "transformation") where these impulses are redirected to the selfless and the holy, so that the animal soul itself loves G-d. See *Tanya*, ch. 27.

This [transformation] is achieved by heeding *these words which I*—the I of "I am who I am"[133]—*command you today;* that which can only be done *today,* the Torah and the *mitzvot* that derive from *sovev.*

MASTERING ONE'S CHARACTER

As a result, man *will know that Havaya is Elokim (The Lord is G-d): Havaya* refers to revelation; *Elokim* to concealment and contraction.[79] We can infer that, just as there is concealment and contraction in the level of *memalei kol almin*—ascents and descents according to the changing of the times, so, too, in the level of *sovev kol almin,* there is *Havaya,* revelation, and *Elokim,* concealment and contraction—when the opposing "other side" becomes powerful.[134]

Therefore, it is necessary to implement the command, *Today, you should know and take to your heart,* through using self-control, and ultimately to master one's character, to finally bring about the fulfillment of the prophecy, *I will remove the spirit of impurity from the land.*[135]

FINAL RESULT

As a result of this, *The earth will be filled with the knowledge of G-d,* and *the land will appease its sin,*[136] meaning that transgressions will become like merits.[137]

(The verse *Today, you should know* is mentioned in the Talmud, in tractates *Rosh Hashanah*[138] and *Gittin*[139]. Also by the *Midrash Rabbah, Va'etchanan,* on the verse *Today, you should know,* and in *Vezot Haberachah* and *Vayikra,* end ch. 6, on the verse (Leviticus 5:1), *And he has witnessed, or seen, or known.*

---

133. See *Ibn Ezra* to Genesis 27:19. In Chasidic terminology, this term refers to *sovev kol almin.* See *Zohar* III:11a—"It is like someone saying 'I am who I am,' and his identity remains unknown." Similarly, when G-d refers to Himself as "I" without a name, the reference is to *sovev kol almin.*

134. As explained in Chapter 5, the energy of *sovev* cannot be fully exposed in the present time, due to the existence of evil. Rather, it exists in a distant and remote manner. It is therefore subject to various modes of exposure, depending on the extent of the existing evil at the time. With the full exposure of *sovev* upon the coming of Moshiach, evil will be erad-

עַל יְדֵי וְהָיוּ הַדְּבָרִים הָאֵלֶּה אֲשֶׁר אָנֹכִי מִי שֶׁאָנֹכִי מְצַוְּךָ הַיּוֹם דַּוְקָא, שֶׁהַתּוֹרָה וְהַמִּצְוֹות הֵם מִבְּחִינַת סוֹבֵב כָּל עָלְמִין,

וְעַל יְדֵי זֶה וְיָדַעְתָּ הַיּוֹם כִּי הוי' הוּא הָאֱלֹהִים, הוי' הוּא בְּחִינַת גִּלּוּי הָאֱלֹהִים בְּחִינַת הֶסְתֵּר וְצִמְצוּם, כִּי כְּמוֹ שֶׁיֵּשׁ בְּחִינַת הֶסְתֵּר וְצִמְצוּם בִּבְחִינַת מְמַלֵּא כָּל עָלְמִין, בְּחִינַת עֲלִיּוֹת וִירִידוֹת לְפִי זְמַנִּים מִתְחַלְּפִים כַּנִּזְכָּר לְעֵיל, כָּךְ יֵשׁ בִּבְחִינַת סוֹבֵב כָּל עָלְמִין, בְּחִינַת הוי' זֶה גִּלּוּי וּבְחִינַת אֱלֹהִים הַיְנוּ הֶסְתֵּר וְצִמְצוּם בְּהִתְגַּבְּרוּת זֶה לְעֻמַּת זֶה,

וְצָרִיךְ לִהְיוֹת וְיָדַעְתָּ הַיּוֹם וַהֲשֵׁבֹתָ אֶל לְבָבֶךָ, בִּבְחִינַת אִתְכַּפְיָא וְאִתְהַפְּכָא, שֶׁיְּקַיֵּם וְאֶת רוּחַ הַטֻּמְאָה אַעֲבִיר מִן הָאָרֶץ,

וְעַל יְדֵי זֶה תִּהְיֶה וּמָלְאָה הָאָרֶץ דֵּעָה וְגוֹ' וְהָאָרֶץ תִּרְצֶה אֶת עֲוֹנָהּ, דְּהַיְנוּ שֶׁזְּדוֹנוֹת יִהְיוּ כִּזְכֻיּוֹת.

(בַּגְּמָרָא נִזְכַּר פָּסוּק וְיָדַעְתָּ הַיּוֹם רֹאשׁ הַשָּׁנָה ל"ב ב' גִּיטִּין נ"ז ב'. רַבּוֹת בְּפָרָשַׁת וָאֶתְחַנַּן עַל פָּסוּק דְּוְיָדַעְתָּ הַיּוֹם. וּבְפָרָשַׁת וְזֹאת הַבְּרָכָה, וְסוֹף פָּרָשַׁת וַיִּקְרָא סוֹף פָּרָשָׁה ו' עַל פָּסוּק וְהוּא עֵד אוֹ רָאָה אוֹ יָדָע.

---

icated permanently. And the discourse concludes that this will be a result of man's initiative in exposing the level of *sovev* in the present time, while the concealment still exists.

135. Zechariah 13:2. Through self-control (*itkafia*) and transforming one's emotions (*it'hapcha*) the person removes the evil from within himself, ultimately causing the evil to be removed from the world at large.

136. Leviticus 26:34, 43.

137. See *Yoma* 86b. The power of re-pentance is so strong that if it is done with the appropriate intensity not only are transgressions pardoned, but are actually transformed into merits. In addition, the deepest and most intimate level of G-d's infinite light (*sovev*) is elicited through repentance. Thus, the future state, when *the earth will be filled with the knowledge of G-d*, sin will be appeased to the point where sins are transformed into merits.

138. 32b.

139. 57b.

[In interpreting the verse, the Midrash states:] *Or seen*—as in the verse, *You have been shown to know [that G-d is our Lord]. Known*—as in the verse, *Today, you should know.*[140]

This Midrash can be explained based on what has been discussed [above, in the discourse]:

You have been shown to know refers to the recognition of *memalei kol almin,* about which it is stated (Job 19:26), *From my flesh I see G-d,* and (Isaiah 40:26) *Lift up your eyes and see [who has created these].* Thus the Midrash states: "Or seen"—as in the verse, *You have been shown.*

The verse *Today, you should know,* on the other hand, refers to the belief and knowledge of *sovev kol almin,* a level which entirely transcends the world. Concerning this level it says, *Today, you should know.* Thus the Midrash states, "Known"—as in the verse, *Today, you should know.*

Hence we find that the first verse of *Shema* contains a large *ayin* and a large *daled* which, together, form the word *eid* (witness), alluding to the concept mentioned by the Midrash[140] that *You are my witnesses,* because *You have been shown to know* and *Today, you should know,* as explained above.

Another interpretation:

The large *ayin* of *Shema* signifies vision[141]—*You have been shown,* while the word *Shema* itself indicates understanding—*Today, you should know.* Thus it is written: *By the testimony of two witnesses shall the matter be established.*[142] *Eidut* (testimony) comprises the same letters as the word *deot* (perceptions). The two witnesses are the two forms of perception—"seeing" and "knowing"—mentioned above. Through them *shall the matter* (דָּבָר) *be established,* referring to the word of G-d (דְּבַר ה׳) which sustains the world. This is alluded to by the large *daled* of the word *Echad.*)

140. *Vayikra Rabbah* 6:5: The complete quote from the Midrash reads: The verse states, *And he has witnessed,*

or seen, or known, yet he did not testify; he shall bear his transgression. "He has witnessed"—refers to the Jewish peo-

אוֹ רָאָה, אַתָּה הָרְאֵתָ לָדַעַת. אוֹ יָדַע, וְיָדַעְתָּ הַיּוֹם.

וְיֵשׁ לְפָרֵשׁ עַל פִּי הָאָמוּר:

דְּפָסוּק אַתָּה הָרְאֵתָ לָדַעַת זֶהוּ עַל בְּחִינַת מְמַלֵּא כָּל עָלְמִין, שֶׁעַל זֶה נֶאֱמַר וּמִבְּשָׂרִי אֶחֱזֶה, שְׂאוּ מָרוֹם עֵינֵיכֶם וּרְאוּ. וְזֶהוּ אוֹ רָאָה. אַתָּה הָרְאֵתָ.

אֲבָל פָּסוּק וְיָדַעְתָּ הַיּוֹם קָאֵי עַל הָאֱמוּנָה וְהַדַּעַת בִּבְחִינַת סוֹבֵב כָּל עָלְמִין, מַה שֶּׁאֵינוּ בְּגֶדֶר עָלְמִין כְּלָל, וְעַל זֶה נֶאֱמַר וְיָדַעְתָּ הַיּוֹם כַּנִּזְכָּר לְעֵיל. וְזֶהוּ אוֹ יָדַע כוּ'.

וְזֶהוּ שֶׁיֵּשׁ בְּפָסוּק רִאשׁוֹן דִּקְרִיאַת שְׁמַע ע' רַבָּתִי וְכֵן ד' דְּאֶחָד, שֶׁהוּא עִנְיַן עֵד, דְּהַיְינוּ בְּחִינַת וְאַתֶּם עֵדַי, כְּמוֹ שֶׁכָּתוּב שָׁם בַּמִּדְרָשׁ, וְהַיְינוּ עַל יְדֵי אַתָּה הָרְאֵתָ לָדַעַת, וְיָדַעְתָּ הַיּוֹם כוּ' וְכַנִּזְכָּר לְעֵיל.

וְגַם יֵשׁ לוֹמַר ע' רַבָּתִי דִּשְׁמַע, עַיִן בְּחִינַת רְאִיָּה הָרְאֵתָ לָדַעַת. וּשְׁמַע לְשׁוֹן הֲבָנָה בְּחִינַת וְיָדַעְתָּ. וְזֶהוּ עַל פִּי שְׁנַיִם עֵדִים יָקוּם דָּבָר, כִּי עֵדוּת אוֹתִיּוֹת דֵעוּת, וּשְׁנַיִם עֵדִים הַיְינוּ בְּחִינַת אוֹ רָאָה אוֹ יָדַע הַנִּזְכָּרִים לְעֵיל, וְעַל יְדֵי זֶה יָקוּם דָּבָר. הוּא בְּחִינַת דְּבַר ה'. וְעַל זֶה מְרַמֵּז הַד' רַבָּתִי דְּאֶחָד):

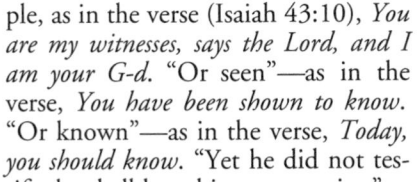

---

ple, as in the verse (Isaiah 43:10), *You are my witnesses, says the Lord, and I am your G-d.* "Or seen"—as in the verse, *You have been shown to know.* "Or known"—as in the verse, *Today, you should know.* "Yet he did not testify, he shall bear his transgression"—

if you do not communicate my sovereignty to the nations I will extract retribution from you.

141. *Ayin* is also the Hebrew word for eye, denoting vision.

142. Deuteronomy 19:15.

BIBLIOGRAPHY

BIBLIOGRAPHY

Asarah Maamarot: Kabbalistic work by R. Menachem Azariah of Fano, Italy (1548-1620).

Avodah Zarah: Talmudic tractate discussing the prohibition on idolatry.

Avot: "Ethics of the Fathers." Talmudic tractate discussing moral and ethical teachings.

Bad Kodesh: Written request to Czar Paul by R. DovBer, second Lubavitcher Rebbe. Includes Introduction by R. Yosef Yitzchak Schneersohn, sixth Lubavitcher Rebbe, and Notes by the Lubavitcher Rebbe, R. Menachem M. Schneerson. New York, 1964.

Bartenura: The primary commentary on the Mishnah by R. Ovadiah of Bartenura (1450-1510). First published in Venice, 1548. Subsequently appears in many editions.

Be'er Hagolah: Explanatory work on the Talmudic and Midrashic Aggadah by R. Yehudah Leow, famed Maharal of Prague (1512-1609), primarily in response to interpretations by the scholar Azariah Min Ha'adumim, in his work *Meor Einayim* (Mantua, 1574). First published in Prague, 1598.

Beit Yosef: Major commentary on R. Yaakov ben Asher's monumental code of Jewish law—the *Tur*—by R. Yosef Karo, author of the *Shulchan Aruch* and one of the foremost authorities on Jewish law.

Berachot: Talmudic tractate addressing the laws of reading the *Shema*, prayer, and blessings.

Bereishit Rabbah: See *Midrash Rabbah*.

Chagigah: Talmudic tractate addressing the laws of the festival sacrifices in the *Beit Hamikdash* and ritual impurity. It also contains many esoteric stories and concepts.

Creation and Redemption: English translation of *Hachodesh Hazeh*

Lachem 5700, delivered by Rabbi Yosef Yitzchak Schneersohn, sixth Lubavitcher Rebbe, on *Shabbat Parashat Tazria, Parashat Hachodesh*, 5700. (Kehot, 2007)

Derech Mitzvotecha: Chasidic work by R. Menachem Mendel Schneersohn, third Lubavitcher Rebbe, author of *Tzemach Tzedek*, offering Chasidic explanations for certain *mitzvot*. Also known as *Taamei Hamitzvot*. Poltava, 1911; Brooklyn, NY, 1953; revised edition, Brooklyn, NY, 1991.

Feminine Faith: English translation of *LeHavin Inyan Rosh Chodesh 5640*, delivered by Rabbi Shmuel Schneersohn, fourth Lubavitcher Rebbe, on *Shabbat Parashat Noach, Rosh Chodesh Marcheshvan*, 5640. (Kehot, 2009)

Gittin: Talmudic tractate discussing the laws of divorce.

Hilchot Beit Habechirah: "Laws of the Chosen House (the *Beit Hamikdash*)" by Maimonides. See *Rambam*.

Hilchot Yesodei HaTorah: "Fundamentals of the Torah" by Maimonides. See *Rambam*.

Horiot: Talmudic tractate discussing the laws of one who disobeys certain rulings of the Jewish High Court of old.

Ibn Ezra: Commentary on the Torah by R. Avraham Ibn Ezra (1080-1164) of Spain, expert grammarian, philosopher, astronomer, mathematician, doctor and poet. Naples, 1488; Constantinople, 1522.

Idra Rabbah; Idra Zutta (pl. Idrot): At times, when the R. Shimon bar Yochai would teach his disciples, they would sit in a circle ("idra," in Aramaic), while he sat in the middle. In these sittings, ten of R. Shimon's students would attend; the group was then called *Idra Rabbah* (the "large group"). Later on, three of the students would leave, and the smaller group, which would have another study session, was called *Idra Zutta* (the "small group"). The sections of the *Zohar* taught at these sessions are termed *Idra Rabbah* (*Zohar* III:127b-145a) and *Idra Zutta* (*Zohar* III:287b-296b).

Iggeret Hakodesh: Letters by R. Schneur Zalman of Liadi published as the fourth section of the *Tanya*.

Jerusalem Talmud: See *Talmud*.

Kiddushin: Talmudic tractate discussing the laws of marriage.

Kilayim: Mishnaic tractate discussing the laws of forbidden mixtures or hybrids of seeds, animals, plants, and clothes.

Likkutei Sichot: Talks delivered and edited by the Lubavitcher Rebbe, Rabbi Menachem M. Schneerson. 39 vols., Brooklyn, NY, 1962-2001.

Likkutei Torah: Chasidic discourses elucidating major themes of the weekly Torah portions and festivals by Rabbi Schneur Zalman of Liadi. Published by his grandson, Rabbi Menachem Mendel Schneersohn, author of *Tzemach Tzedek*. Zhitomir, 1848; Munich, 1948; Brooklyn, NY, 1965; 1999. See *Torah Or*.

Maamarei Admur HaEmtza'ee, Hanachot 5577: Transcriber's record of Chasidic discourses delivered by R. DovBer, second Lubavitcher Rebbe, during the year 5577 (1817).

Maamarei Admur Hazaken 5566: Chasidic discourses delivered by R. Schneur Zalman of Liadi during the year 5566 (1805-1806). 2 vols., Brooklyn, NY, 2004-2005.

Maharzav: Commentary on *Midrash Rabbah* by R. Zev Wolf Einhorn of Horodna, Poland (d. 1862), printed in the standard editions of the Midrash with commentaries.

Matnot Kehunah: A commentary appearing in nearly every edition of the *Midrash*, by Rabbi Yissachar Naftali HaKohen Ashkenazi (16th-17th Century); student of R. Moshe Isserles.

Megillah: Talmudic tractate addressing the laws and story of Purim, as well as laws of Torah reading and the synagogue.

Midrash Rabbah: A major collection of homilies and commentaries on the Torah, attributed to Rabbi Oshaya Rabbah (circa. 3rd century); some place it as a work of the early Gaonic period. This work covers the Five Books of Moses and the Five *Megillot*.

Moreh Nevuchim: "Guide for the Perplexed." One of the most important works on Jewish philosophy, by R. Moshe ben Maimon (Maimonides).

Mystical Concepts in Chasidism: Guide to the intricate concepts of Jewish mysticism found in Chabad Chasidic philosophy. Authored by Rabbi J. Immanuel Schochet (Kehot, 1988).

Or Hatorah: Chasidic discourses on Scripture by R. Menachem Mendel of Lubavitch, author of *Tzemach Tzedek*. Berditchev, 1913; Brooklyn, NY, 1950 and on.

Or Torah: Compilation of Chasidic teachings by R. DovBer, the Maggid of Mezritch and leader of the second generation of Chasidism. Compiled by his students, this work provides unique insight into various concepts contained in Scripture, Talmud, and Kabbalah, through the Chasidic lens. First printed in Koretz, 1804. New, revised edition, Brooklyn, NY, 2006.

Pardes (Pardes Rimonim): See *Ramak*.

Pesachim: Talmudic tractate discussing the Passover laws.

Pirkei d'Rabbi Eliezer: A Midrash authored by the second century Mishnaic Sage, Rabbi Eliezer ben Horkenus, also known as Rabbi Eliezer Hagadol ("the great"). "The earliest of all Tannaic treatises, revealed and famous in the era of our authoritative Rabbis and mystical Kabbalists, the *Rishonim*, who used and benefited from its light" (—from the title page).

Rabbenu Yonah: R. Yonah ben Avraham of Gerona (d. 1263), teacher of Rashba. Author of classic ethical works and a commentary on the Talmud.

Ramak: Acronym for R. Moshe Cordovero (1522-1570). Leader of a prominent Kabbalistic school in Safed; author of the Kabbalistic *Pardes Rimonim, Elima Rabbati, Shiur Komah, Or Ne'erav*, the ethical *Tomer Devorah*, and many other works.

Rambam: Acronym for R. Moshe ben Maimon (1135-1204), also known as Maimonides. Regarded as one of Judaism's foremost Torah authorities, he authored, among other works, *Mishneh Torah*, a phenomenal redaction of the entire Talmud.

Ramban: Acronym for R. Moshe ben Nachman (1194–1270), also known as Nachmanides. Kabbalist and author, he composed numerous works, including commentaries on the Torah and the Talmud, *Milchamot Hashem, Sefer Hagemul, Sefer Havikuach,* and *Sefer Hageulah*.

Rashi: Acronym for R. Shlomo Yitzchaki. Rabbi Shlomo ben Yitzchak lived in Troyes, France and Worms, Germany (1040-1105). His commentary is printed in practically all editions of the Torah and Talmud, and is the subject of some two hundred commentators. With regard to his commentary on *Avot*, R. Yaakov Emden in his *Lechem Shamayim* (Amsterdam, 1751) asserts that although attributed to Rashi could not have been written by Rashi.

Rosh Hashanah: Talmudic tractate discussing the laws of the Rosh Hashanah festival and the Jewish calendar.

Sefer Halikkutim: Collection of concepts explained in Chasidic teachings, culled from the works by R. Menachem Mendel of Lubavitch, author of *Tzemach Tzedek*. Arranged in encyclopedic form according to the *alef-beit*, it also contains references to the works of the other Chabad Rebbes for the respective topics. 22 vols., Brooklyn, NY, 1977-84.

Sefer Hamaamarim 5680-5710: Set of Chasidic discourses delivered by Rabbi Yosef Yitzchak Schneersohn, sixth Lubavitcher Rebbe, between 5680-5710 (1920-1950), the years of his leadership; nineteen volumes.

Sefer Hamaamarim Melukat: Chasidic discourses delivered and edited by the Lubavitcher Rebbe, Rabbi Menachem M. Schneerson, during the course of his leadership 5711-5752 (1951-1992). Six vols., Brooklyn, NY, 1987-1992.

Sefer Yetzirah: One of the oldest written sources of Kabbalah, it is attributed to the Patriarch Abraham. It has been the subject of over one hundred commentaries since it was first published in Mantua, 1562.

Shaar Hayichud v'haEmunah: Second part of *Tanya*; explores the doctrines of Divine Unity, Providence and faith.

Shaar Maamarei Rashbi: Section of a compilation of the Arizal's Kabbalistic teachings, by his primary disciple and exponent, Rabbi Chaim Vital (1543–1620).

Shabbat: Talmudic tractate discussing the laws of Shabbat.

Shaloh: Monumental work by R. Yeshayah HaLevi Horowitz (1558-1628), chief rabbi of Prague. An acronym for *Shnei Luchot Habrit*, *Shaloh* contains explanations and commentaries on the profound aspects of the Torah, *mitzvot*, the festivals, Jewish customs and the fundamental beliefs of Judaism, including basic instruction in Kabbalah. First published in Amsterdam, 1648.

Shir Hashirim Rabbah: See *Midrash Rabbah*.

Shulchan Aruch: Code of Jewish Law by R. Yosef Karo (1488-1575), one of the foremost authorities on Jewish law. Consisting of four parts, *Orach Chaim, Yoreh Deah, Choshen Mishpat,* and *Even Ha'ezer,* it later became the standard work of Jewish law for all Jews. First published in Venice, 1564.

Talmud: The embodiment of the Oral Law. Following the codification of the Mishnah by Rabbi Yehudah Hanassi, c. 150 c.e., later discussions, known as the Talmud, were redacted in two parts. The more popular Babylonian Talmud was compiled by Rav Ashi and Ravina (about the end of the fifth century, c.e.). The Jerusalem Talmud was compiled by Rabbi Yochanan bar Nappacha (about the end of the third century, c.e.).

Tanya: Philosophical magnum opus by R. Schneur Zalman of Liadi, in which the principles of Chabad are expounded. The name is derived from the initial word of this work. Also called *Likkutei Amarim*, this work was first published in Slavita, 1797, and has seen over 5000 editions. Hebrew-English bi-lingual edition first printed in London, 1973.

Tikkunei Zohar: A work of seventy chapters on the first word of the Torah, by the school of R. Shimon bar Yochai (circa. 120 c.e.). First printed in Mantua, 1558, *Tikkunei Zohar* contains some of the most important discussions in *Kabbalah*, and is essential for understanding the *Zohar*.

Torah Or: Chasidic discourses elucidating major themes of the weekly Torah portions and festivals by Rabbi Schneur Zalman of Liadi. Published by his grandson, Rabbi Menachem Mendel Schneersohn, author of *Tzemach Tzedek*. Kopust, 1837; Munich, 1948; Brooklyn, NY, 1955; 1991. See *Likkutei Torah*.

Torat Shmuel—Sefer 5627: Chasidic discourses delivered by R. Shmuel Schneersohn, fourth Lubavitcher Rebbe, during the year 5627 (1866-1867). Brooklyn, NY, 2000.

Tur: Two works by this name were authored by R. Yaakov ben Asher. One, a code of Jewish law—called *Arbaah Turim*—was first published in Piove di Sacco, 1475. The other, a commentary on the Torah called *Baal Haturim*, first appeared in Constantinople, 1514.

True Existence: English translation of *Mi Chamocha, 5629*, a Chasidic discourse delivered by R. Shmuel Schneersohn, fourth Lubavitcher Rebbe, on *Shabbat Parashat Yitro and Shabbat Parashat Shemini*, 5629 (Kehot, 2002).

Vayikra Rabbah: See *Midrash Rabbah*.

Yoma: Talmudic tractate discussing the laws of Yom Kippur and the Yom Kippur service in the *Beit Hamikdash*.

Zohar: Basic work of Kabbalah compiled by the Mishnaic sage, R. Shimon bar Yochai, in Hebrew and Aramaic as a commentary on the Torah.

INDEX

INDEX

OTHER TITLES IN
THE CHASIDIC HERITAGE SERIES

Rabbi Schneur Zalman of Liadi

THE ETERNAL BOND *from Torah Or*

Translated by Rabbi Ari Sollish

This discourse explores the spiritual significance of *brit milah*, analyzing two dimensions in which our connection with G-d may be realized. For in truth, there are two forms of spiritual circumcision. Initially, man must "circumcise his heart," freeing himself to the best of his ability from his negative, physical drives; ultimately, though, it is G-d who truly liberates man from his material attachment.

જ઼જ઼જ઼

JOURNEY OF THE SOUL from *Torah Or*

Translated by Rabbi Ari Sollish

Drawing upon the parallel between Queen Esther's impassioned plea to King Ahasuerus for salvation and the soul's entreaty to G-d for help in its spiritual struggle, this discourse examines the root of the soul's exile, and the dynamics by which it lifts itself from the grip of materialism and ultimately finds a voice with which to express its G-dly yearnings. Includes a brief biography of the author.

જ઼જ઼જ઼

TRANSFORMING THE INNER SELF from *Likkutei Torah*

Translated by Rabbi Chaim Zev Citron

This discourse presents a modern-day perspective on the Biblical command to offer animal sacrifices. Rabbi Schneur Zalman teaches that each of us possesses certain character traits that can be seen as "animalistic," or materialistic, in nature, which can lead a person toward a life of material indulgence. Our charge, then, is to "sacrifice" and transform the animal within, to refine our animal traits and utilize them in our pursuit of spiritual perfection.

જ઼જ઼જ઼

Rabbi DovBer of Lubavitch

FLAMES from *Shaarei Orah*
Translated by Dr. Naftoli Loewenthal
This discourse focuses on the multiple images of the lamp, the oil, the wick and the different hues of the flame in order to express profound guidance in the Divine service of every individual. Although *Flames* is a Chanukah discourse, at the same time, it presents concepts that are of perennial significance. Includes the first English biography of the author ever published.

Rabbi Menachem Mendel of Lubavitch,
the Tzemach Tzedek

THE MITZVAH TO LOVE YOUR FELLOW AS YOURSELF
from *Derech Mitzvotecha*
Translated by Rabbis Nissan Mangel and Zalman I. Posner
The discourse discusses the Kabbalistic principle of the "collective soul of the world of *Tikkun*" and explores the essential unity of all souls. The discourse develops the idea that when we connect on a soul level, we can love our fellow as we love ourselves; for in truth, we are all one soul. Includes a brief biography of the author.

Rabbi Shmuel of Lubavitch

TRUE EXISTENCE
Mi Chamocha 5629
Translated by Rabbis Yosef Marcus and Avraham D. Vaisfiche
This discourse revolutionizes the age-old notion of Monotheism, i.e., that there is no other god besides Him. Culling from Talmudic and Midrashic sources, the discourse makes the case that not only is there no other god besides Him, there is nothing besides Him—literally. The only thing that truly exists is G-d. Includes a brief biography of the author.

᪥᪥᪥

TRUE EXISTENCE *The Chasidic View of Reality*
A Video-CD with Rabbi Manis Friedman
Venture beyond science and Kabbalah and discover the world of
Chasidism. This Video-CD takes the viewer step-by-step through
the basic Chasidic and Kabbalistic view of creation and existence.
In clear, lucid language, Rabbi Manis Friedman deciphers these eso-
teric concepts and demonstrates their modern-day applications.

CHANNELING THE DIVINE
Itta B'Midrash Tillim
Edited by Rabbi Avraham D. Vaisfiche
The Bar Mitzvah, the day a Jewish boy turns thirteen, is a turning
point in his life. He comes of age, becoming responsible for adher-
ence to the *mitzvot* and fully accountable for his actions—and
everyone celebrates. Chabad Chasidim mark this milestone by having the "Bar Mitzvah boy" publicly deliver a discourse, originally
delivered by Rabbi Shalom DovBer Schneersohn, fifth Lubavitcher
Rebbe, on the occasion of his Bar Mitzvah in 5634 (1873). Its main
theme is the cosmic impact of performing the mitzvah of *tefillin*,
and the special connection between this mitzvah and the age of Bar
Mitzvah.

FEMININE FAITH
L'Havin Inyan Rosh Chodesh, 5640
Translated by Rabbi Shais Taub
When the Jews served the Golden Calf during their sojourn in the
wilderness, says the Midrash, the women refused to join them.
Feminine Faith traces the roots of the feminine within the supernal-
realms, and explores its relationship to women and how it translated into their aversion for unholy and ungodly worship. Why are-
women more sensitive than men to G-d's role in earthly events and
His mastery over Creation? In this discourse, Rabbi Shmuel
Schneersohn, fourth leader of Chabad Lubavitch (1834-1882),
explores G-d's unity and immanence in the world, and the innate
sensitivity that women posses to spirituality.

Rabbi Shalom DovBer of Lubavitch

YOM TOV SHEL ROSH HASHANAH 5659
Discourse One
Translated by Rabbis Yosef Marcus and Moshe Miller
The discourse explores the attribute of *malchut* and the power of speech while introducing some of the basic concepts of Chasidism and Kabbalah in a relatively easy to follow format. Despite its title and date of inception, the discourse is germane throughout the year. Includes a brief biography of the author.

~<~<~<

FORCES IN CREATION
Yom Tov Shel Rosh Hashanah 5659 Discourse Two
Translated by Rabbis Moshe Miller and Shmuel Marcus
A fascinating journey beyond the terrestrial, into the myriad spiritual realms that shape our existence. Rabbi Shalom DovBer systematically traces the origins of earth, Torah and souls, drawing the reader higher and higher into the mystical, cosmic dimensions that lie beyond the here and now, and granting a deeper awareness of who we are at our core.

~<~<~<

THE POWER OF RETURN
Yom Tov Shel Rosh Hashanah 5659 Discourse Three
Translated by Rabbi Y. Eliezer Danzinger
This discourse examines the inner workings of *teshuvah*, and explains how it is precisely through making a detailed and honest examination of one's character and spiritual standing—which inevitably leads one to a contrite and broken heart—that allows one to realize his or her essential connection with G-d.

~<~<~<

TRACT ON PRAYER

Kuntres Ha Tefillah
Translated by Rabbi Y. Eliezer Danzinger
Tract on Prayer expounds on the concept of *tefillah*—prayer, as understood in Chabad Chasidic philosophy. Building on the Talmudic dictum that prayer constitutes the "service of the heart," *Tract on Prayer* captures the quintessence of *tefillah* as the vehicle for attaining attachment to G-d. It guides the worshiper in preparing for this divine service of the heart, setting out the role and dynamics of contemplation before and during prayer. *Tract on Prayer* also explores various Kabbalistic and Chasidic concepts.

৵৵৵

OVERCOMING FOLLY

Kuntres Umaayan Mibeit Hashem
Translated by Rabbi Zalman I. Posner
In this classis ethico-philosophical work, Rabbi Shalom DovBer weaves Chasidic doctrine, Kabbalah thoughts, Biblical and Talmudic texts and candid insights into human frailties into a document structured and systematic, yet informal and personal—a text for study and meditation.

৵৵৵

THE SIMPLE SERVANT

UMikneh Rav 5666
Translated by Rabbi Yosef Marcus
This discourse elaborates upon three types of personalities with distinct approaches to Divine service: 1) The child of G-d, naturally committed; 2) The loyal servant of G-d, motivated by his appreciation of G-d; 3) The simple servant of G-d, driven by his acceptance of the yoke of Heaven. His apathy makes serving G-d difficult. Yet he does his work consistently because he is reaching beyond himself—overcoming his own nature.

Rabbi Yosef Yitzchak of Lubavitch

THE PRINCIPLES OF EDUCATION AND GUIDANCE
Klalei Hachinuch Vehahadrachah
Translated by Rabbi Y. Eliezer Danzinger
The Principles of Education and Guidance is a compelling treatise that examines the art of educating. In this thought-provoking analysis, Rabbi Yosef Yitzchak teaches how to assess the potential of any pupil, how to objectively evaluate one's own strengths, and how to successfully use reward and punishment—methods that will help one become a more effective educator.

⋄⋄⋄

THE FOUR WORLDS
Translated by Rabbis Yosef Marcus and Avraham D. Vaisfiche
Overview by Rabbi J. Immanuel Schochet
At the core of our identity is the desire to be one with our source, and to know the spiritual realities that give our physical life the transcendental importance of the Torah's imperatives. In this letter to a yearning Chasid, the Rebbe explains the mystical worlds of *Atzilut, Beriah, Yetzirah,* and *Asiyah.*

⋄⋄⋄

ONENESS IN CREATION
Kol Hamaarich B'Echad 5690
Translated by Rabbi Y. Eliezer Danzinger
Said by Rabbi Yosef Yitzchak at the close of his 1930 visit to Chicago, this discourse explores the concept of Divine Unity as expressed in the first verse of the *Shema.* The discourse maintains that it is a G-dly force that perpetually sustains all of creation. As such, G-d is one with creation. And it is our study of Torah and performance of the mitzvot that reveals this essential oneness.

⋄⋄⋄

CREATION AND REDEMPTION
Hachodesh 5700
Translated by Rabbi Yosef Marcus
Tishrei celebrates Creation, the birth of the world, indicative of the natural order. Nissan commemorates the miraculous Exodus from Egypt, or the supernatural. In human terms, when struggling with the obfuscation of the natural, the key is to recognize the dimension where the limitations of the natural order do not exist. In fact, the physical exists only so that we may demonstrate how it too exposes the Divine truth. And when we recognize this, we can realize the supernatural even within the natural.

৵৵৵

THE MAJESTIC BRIDE
Lecha Dodi 5689 / 5714
Translated by Rabbis Ari Sollish and Avraham D. Vaisfiche
Customarily recited by a groom at the Kabbalat Panim reception, *Lecha Dodi* traces the Kabbalistic meaning of the order of the wedding ceremony, when first the guests welcome the groom, and then walk with the groom to welcome the bride, at which point the groom covers the bride's face with the veil. The discourse cites a number of examples and other situations where similar procedures occur, finally applying the reasoning to groom and bride to understand the Kabbalat Panim ceremony and the purpose of marriage.

Rabbi Menachem M. Schneerson,
the Lubavitcher Rebbe

FULL DEVOTION
Lo Tihyeh Meshakelah 5712
Translated by Rabbi Zalman Abraham
Referred to as a landmark discourse, delivered by the Rebbe barely two years after ascending to the leadership of Chabad-Lubavitch, this discourse is perhaps unique among all of the Rebbe's teachings in the sense that its message required a retooling of our conception of divine service. It discusses the self-satisfaction that might result from our love and awe of G-d, and that contemplating the fact that our days upon earth need to be utilized to the fullest serves to remove any such feelings of satisfaction.

THE PATH TO SELFLESSNESS
Yehudah Atah 5738
Translated by Rabbi Shmuel Simpson

Beginning with the words *Yehuda Atah*, the discourse examines the blessing which Yaakov blessed his fourth son, Yehuda, as compared to the blessings he gave his first three sons, Reuven, Shimon and Levi. Yaakov's sons embody distinctive forms of divine service, which correspond to distinct sections of the prayers of Shema and the Amidah. Using these distinctions, the discourse further derives lessons about the bond between the individual Jewish soul and G-d.

§-§-§

NURTURING FAITH
Kuntres Purim Kattan 5752
Translated by Rabbi Yosef Marcus

At its core, this discourse discusses the function of a *nassi*, a Jewish leader, who awakens within every single person the deepest part of the soul. Similar to Moses, the *nassi* inspires the person so that one's most basic faith in G-d leaves the realm of the abstract and becomes real. *Nurturing Faith* will cultivate your bond with the Rebbe's role as the Moses of our generation.

§-§-§

STAYING THE COURSE
a collection of discourses by the Chabad Rebbes on the inseparable bond between Rebbe and Chasid
Translated by Rabbi Shmuel Simpson

Discussing various ways through which the Chasid can continue to nurture and renew this bond, the discourses presented in this work speak to the seasoned Chasid as well as those newly introduced to the Rebbe and his teachings.

There are many important manuscripts
that are ready to go to press, but are
waiting for a sponsor like you.

Please consider one of these opportunities
and make an everlasting contribution to
Jewish scholarship and Chasidic life.

For more information please contact:

The Chasidic Heritage Series
770 Eastern Parkway
Brooklyn, New York 11213
Tel: 718.774.4000
E-mail: info@kehot.com

COMING SOON!

PADAH BESHALOM 5668
By Rabbi Shalom DovBer of Lubavitch
Translated by Rabbi Zalman Abraham

KOL PRUTA
By Rabbi Menachem Mendel of Lubavitch, author of *Tzemach Tzedek*
Translated by Rabbi Shmuel Simpson

הוצאת ספרים
קרני הוד תורה
ליובאוויטש